Just Look and Cook

A visual guide of easy recipes for everyone

The Text Free Way

Foreword by Neven Maguire

As a chef who started cooking at 12 years of age, I'm delighted to see a book such as this in the marketplace! They say a picture paints a thousand words, and this is certainly the case for the Just Look and Cook Cookbook.

The range of recipes, coupled with the user friendly style of the book will appeal to so many groups of people including college students, teenagers, beginner cooks and those who prefer to cook just what they see! This book will help all those with literacy and learning difficulties to cook mouth-watering, yet simple and economical recipes for themselves.

I love the fact that the book brings cooking back to its most basic format, often relying on instinct rather than exact measurements or cooking terminology. I'm certainly looking forward to trying a recipe or two from it myself!

I wish Eileen Kirrane the very best of luck in this endeavour.

Neven

Designed and Published by Riverhouse Books
Visit www.justlookandcook.ie

First published in Sligo (March 2013) by Riverhouse Books.

ISBN: 978-0-9575789-0-6

Artwork by JDK Design.
Photography by James Fraher.

Printed in Ireland on FSC-certified paper for Riverhouse Books.

Acknowledgements

I am blessed to be a part of a large extended family that live here, there and everywhere and to now having a gang of my own, who make my life complete. You all mean the world to me.

It is not every day a person publishes their first book, so I am taking this opportunity to thank a lot of people who assisted me along the way.

JP - You have been by my side every step of this journey keeping me motivated.

Jonathan - For inspiring me and proving to me this book was worth all the effort.

Debbie - You took on the role of constructive critic reluctantly but did it in the nicest possible way.

David - For the keen eye while you were proof reading and for believing in the book.

Jason - Budding chef and great photographer's assistant during the days of the photo shoot.

Justin - Thank you for the listening ear, helpful advice and the business cards.

Rachel - Bun maker extraordinaire! I'll leave that job to you in the future.

My little grandson Adam - Who can eat more of Granny's pancakes than seems possible.

Brian - You have the hands of a model and always remember, the timer is not an alarm clock!

Kelly Coleman - For taking the time out to cook some of the recipes for me.

Anne Kelly AKGMS - More than a mentor, your constant guidance above and beyond the call of duty made you an integral part of this book coming alive. Thank you for your belief in my book and in me.

Also my thanks go to the following who tried and tested recipes, including Men's Sheds Tubbercurry, Cloonacool National School, St. Attracta's Community School, Deirdre, St. Joseph's Special School, National Learning Network, Acquired Brain Injury Ireland, Gallagher House, Tubbercurry, Training Centre & Resource Centre Sligo.

A special thanks to all the lovely ladies and students of Autism Services who I had the privilege to work with over the last few months. Loved every minute of it guys!

Thanks also to Sligo County Enterprise Board and FÁS for your assistance in providing mentoring services and courses, to Don at IT Sligo Students Union, to Cathy Adult Literacy Organiser Sligo and to Tubbercurry Family Resource Centre for your kindness and use of your kitchen facilities.

My thanks to my hand models, David, Debbie, JP, Brian and Rachel.

Special thanks to Neven Maguire for taking time out of your busy schedule to write the foreword for me. It is greatly appreciated.

A final thanks go to Jeff at JDK Design and James Fraher, Photographer in your help in bringing this book to print.

Just Look and Cook – The Recipes

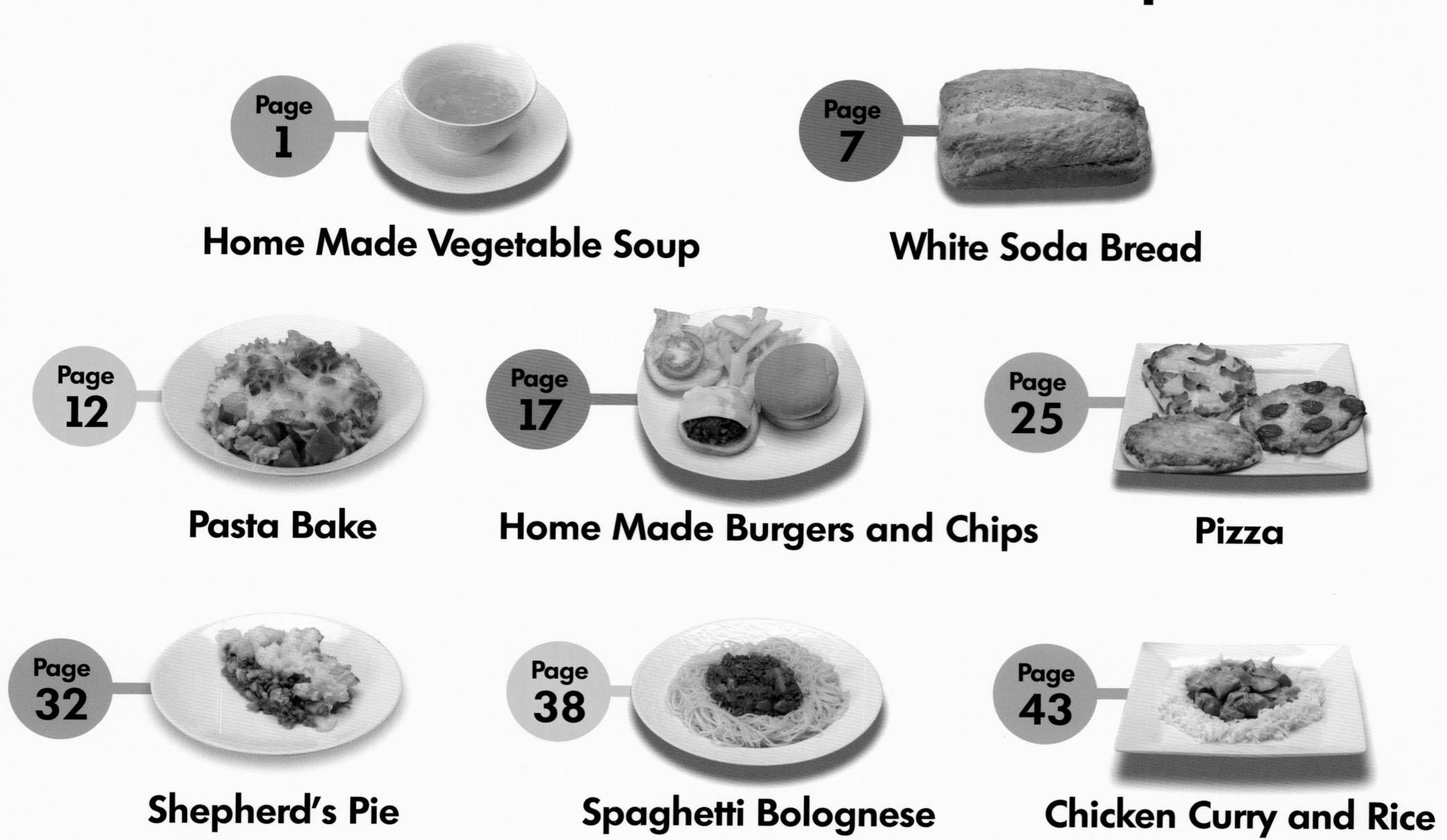

Page 49
Chicken Maryland
Page 49
Chicken Fillet Burger
Page 49
Chicken Fillet Roll
Page 54
Pancakes
Page 58
Scrambled Egg and Toast
Page 62
French Toast
Page 66
Apple Crumble and Custard
Page 70
Strawberry Cheesecake
Page 75
Buns

Home Made Vegetable Soup

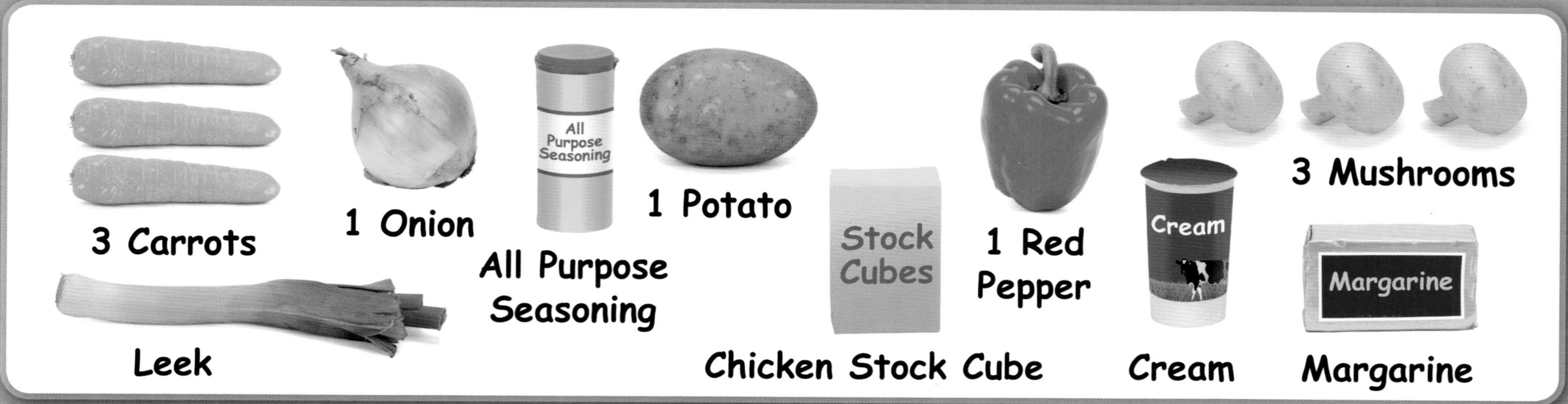
All Purpose Seasoning
Stock Cubes
Cream
Margarine
3 Carrots
1 Onion
All Purpose Seasoning
1 Potato
1 Red Pepper
3 Mushrooms
Leek
Chicken Stock Cube
Cream
Margarine

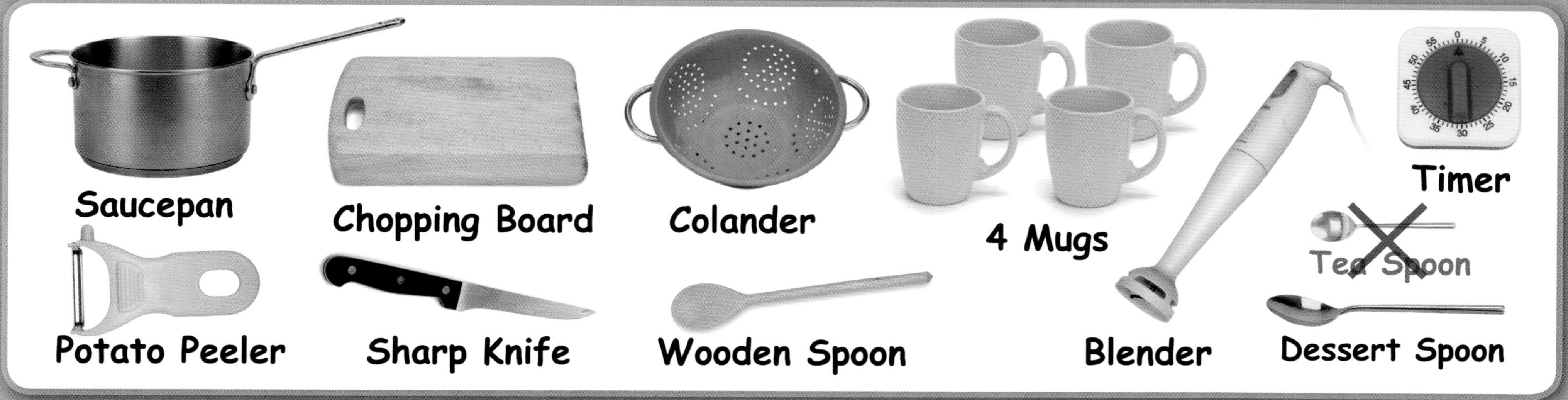
Saucepan
Chopping Board
Colander
4 Mugs
Timer
Tea Spoon
Potato Peeler
Sharp Knife
Wooden Spoon
Blender
Dessert Spoon

Home Made Vegetable Soup

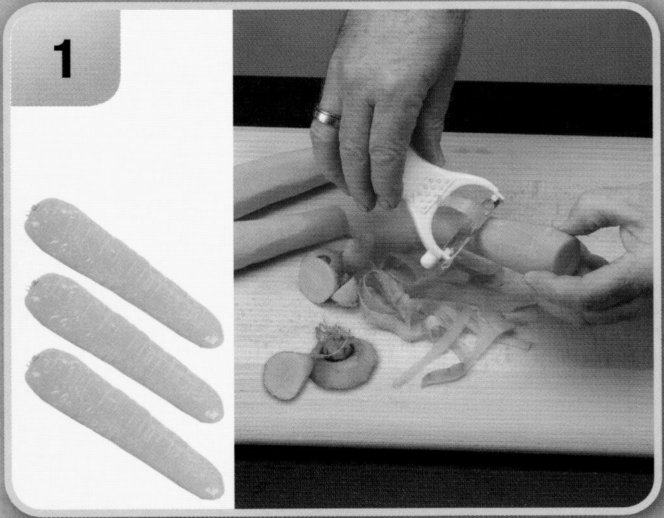

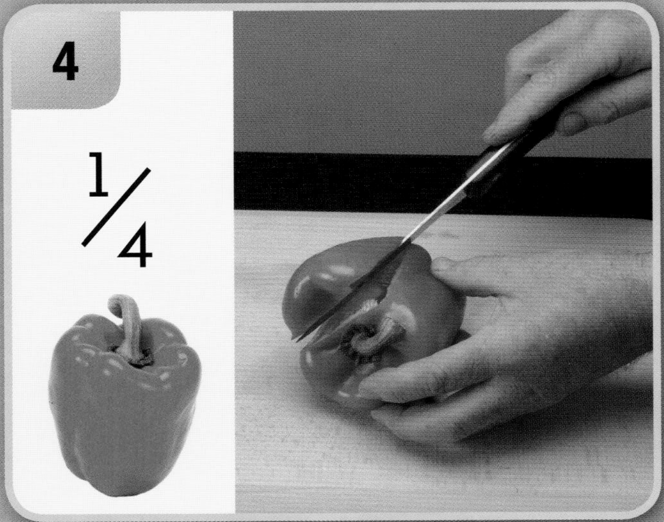

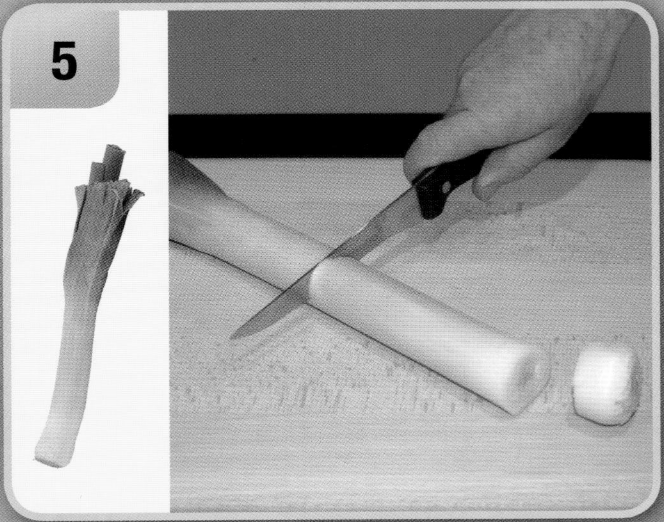

Home Made Vegetable Soup

7

8

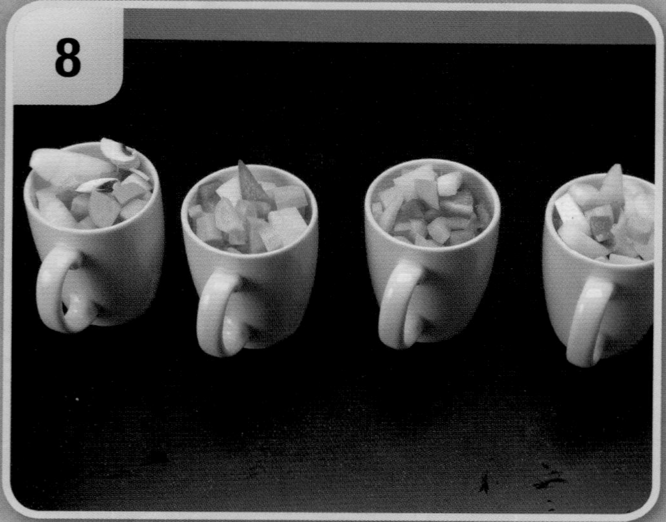

9

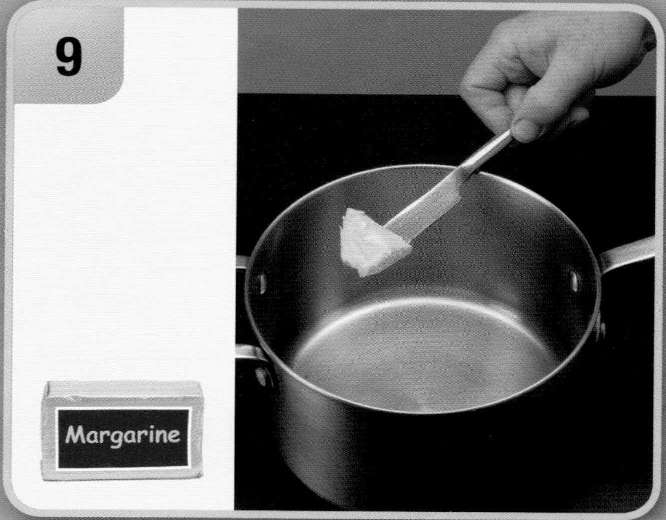

10

11

12

Home Made Vegetable Soup

Home Made Vegetable Soup

19

20

21

22

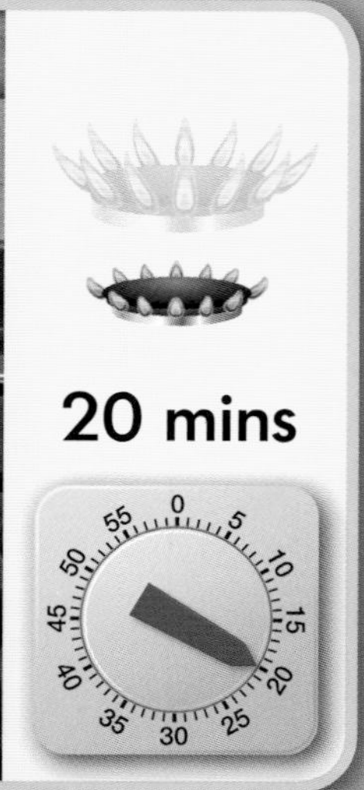

23

24

Home Made Vegetable Soup

White Soda Bread

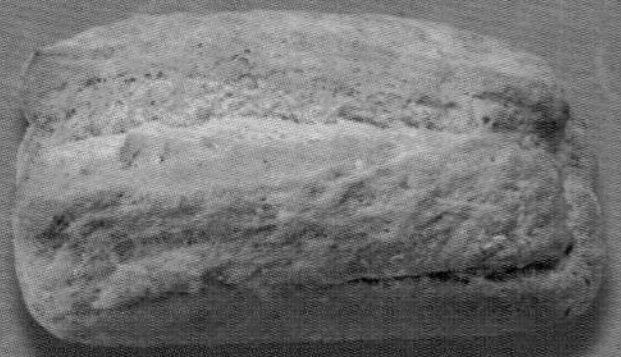

Plain Flour

Bread Soda

Margarine

Sugar

Cream of Tartar

Low Fat Milk

Salt

Butter Knife

Tea Spoon

Timer

Sieve

Mixing Bowl

~~Dessert Spoon~~

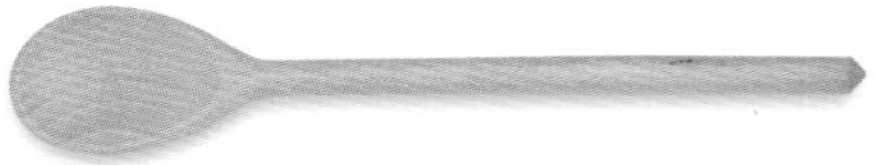

Wooden Spoon

2lb Loaf Tin

3 Mugs

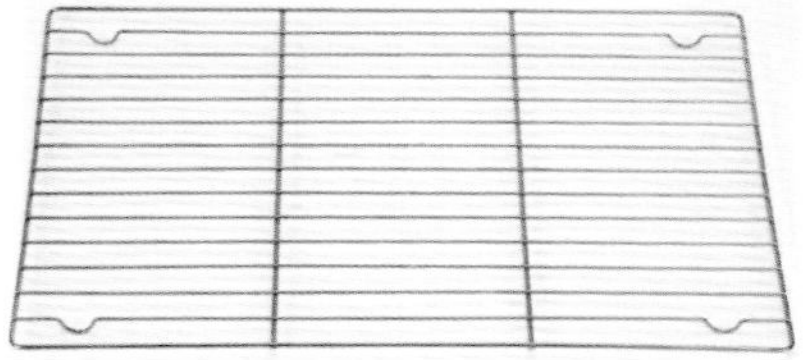

Wire Tray

White Soda Bread

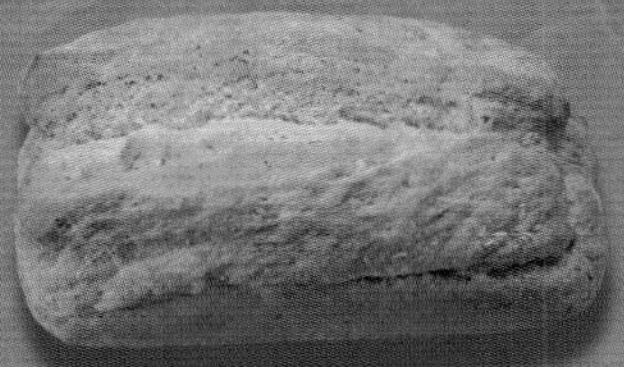

1

200°C 400°F Gas mark 6

2

3

4

5

6

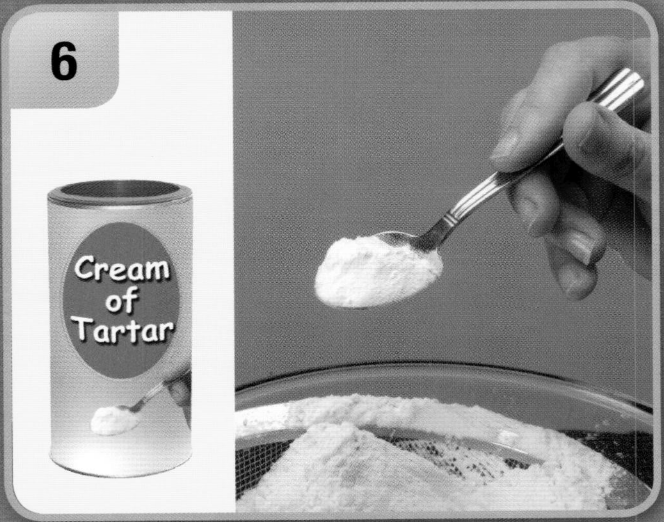

White Soda Bread

White Soda Bread

13

14

15

16

17

White Soda Bread

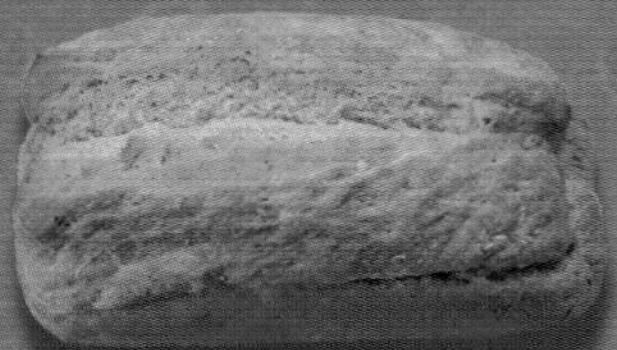

18

19

20

21

22

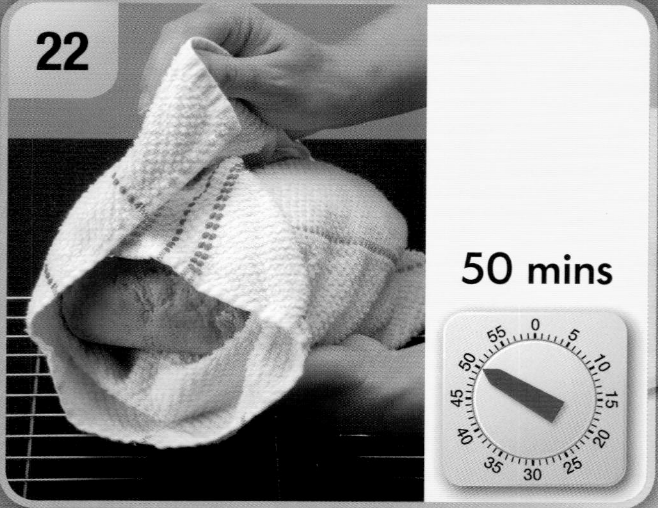

Pasta Bake

Oil

1 Onion

1 Red Pepper

Fusilli Pasta

Jar of Creamy Tomato Pasta Bake

Mushrooms

Grated Cheese

Saucepan

Chopping Board

Tea Spoon

Dessert Spoon

Sharp Knife

Spatula

Frying Pan

Colander

Timer

Oven Dish

3 Mugs

Pasta Bake

1

200°C 400°F Gas mark 6

2

3

1/2

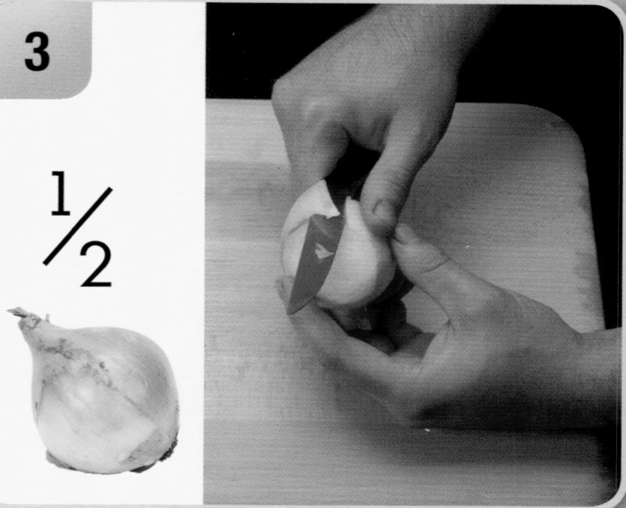

4

1/2

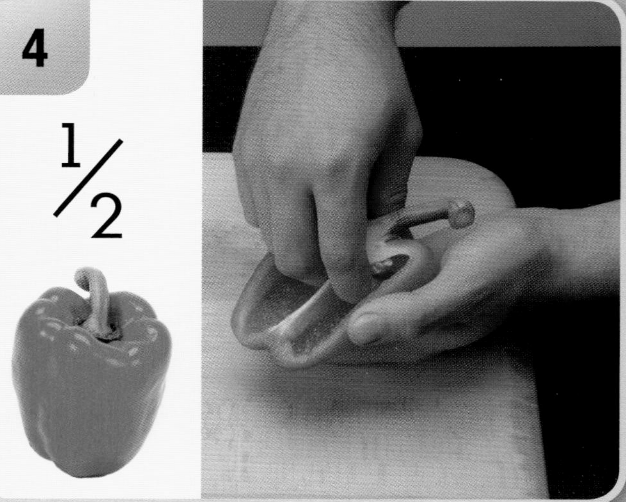

5

6

Full Mug

Pasta Bake

7

8

9

10

11

12

Pasta Bake

13

14

15

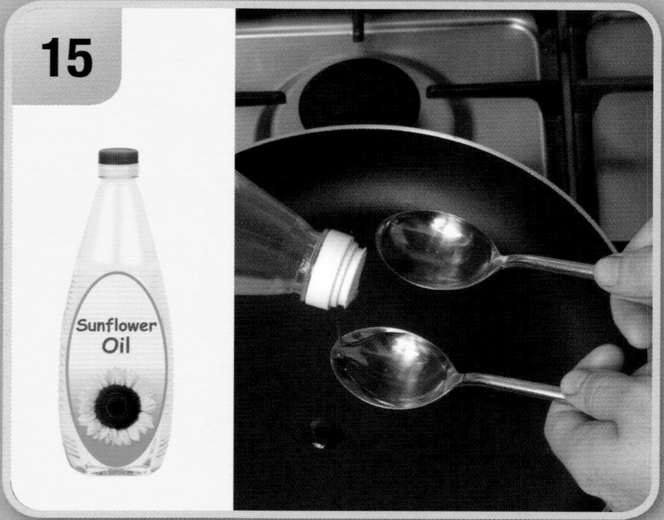

16

17

18

Pasta Bake

19

20

21

22

23

Fork Potato Peeler Timer Mug 2 Oven Trays Spatula Bowl Dessert Spoon

Wooden Spoon Rolling Pin Colander Sharp Knife Frying Pan ~~Tea Spoon~~ Chopping Board

Tomato Ketchup 4 Potatoes 1 Onion Cheese Slices Burger Buns Tomato Puree 6 Eggs

1 Tomato Lettuce Oil Plain Flour Salt & Black Pepper 500g Mince

Home Made Burgers and Chips

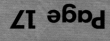

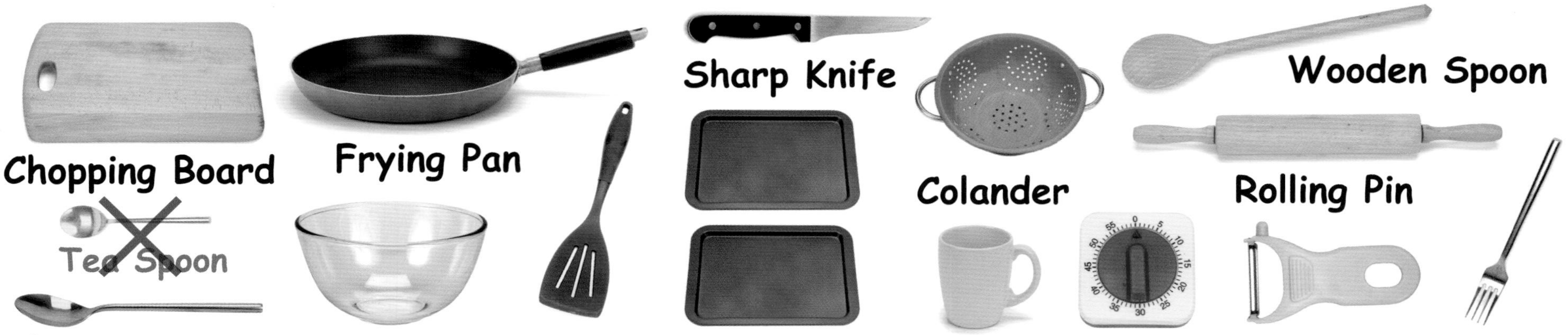

Home Made Burgers and Chips

1

2

3

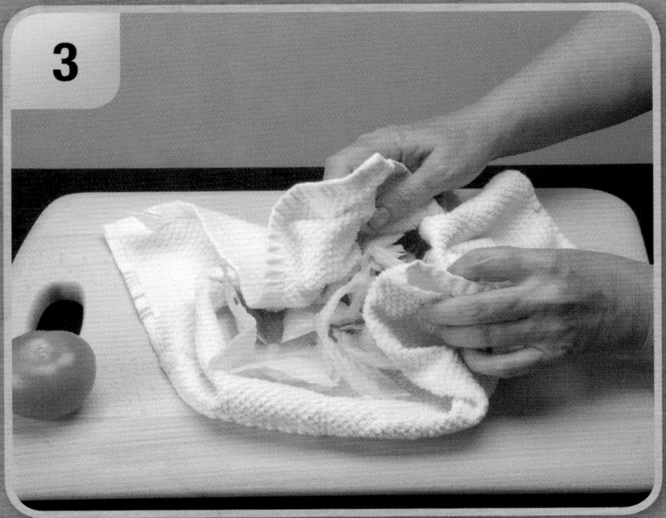

4

5

6

Home Made Burgers and Chips

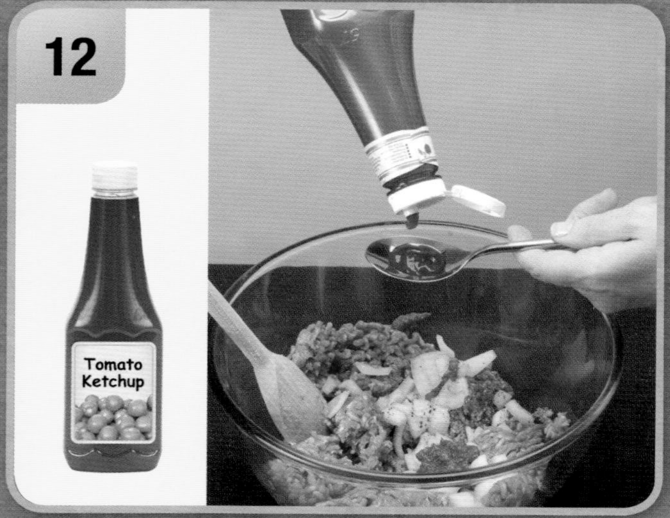

Home Made Burgers and Chips

13

14

15

16

17

18

Home Made Burgers and Chips

19

20

21

22

23

Home Made Burgers and Chips

Home Made Burgers and Chips

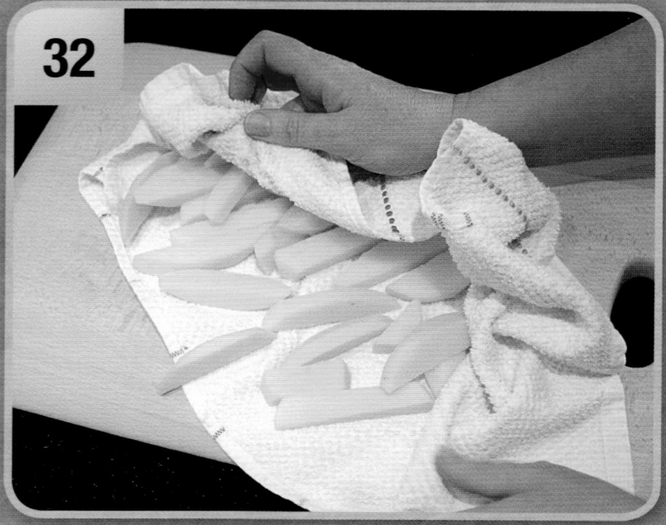

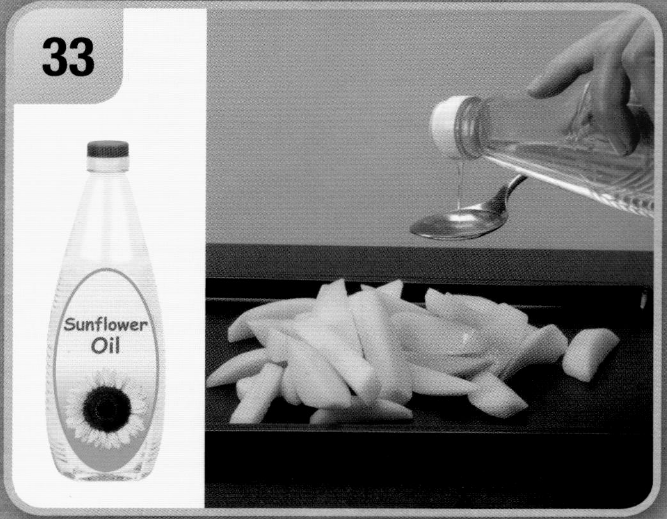

Home Made Burgers and Chips

36

37

38

39

Pizza

Oil
Sunflower Oil
Plain Flour
Plain Flour
Salt
SALT
Grated Cheese
Grated Cheese
Tomato Puree
Tomato Purée
Toppings:
Packet Ham
Ham
Tin of Pineapple
Pineapple
Chorizo Sausage
Chorizo Sausage

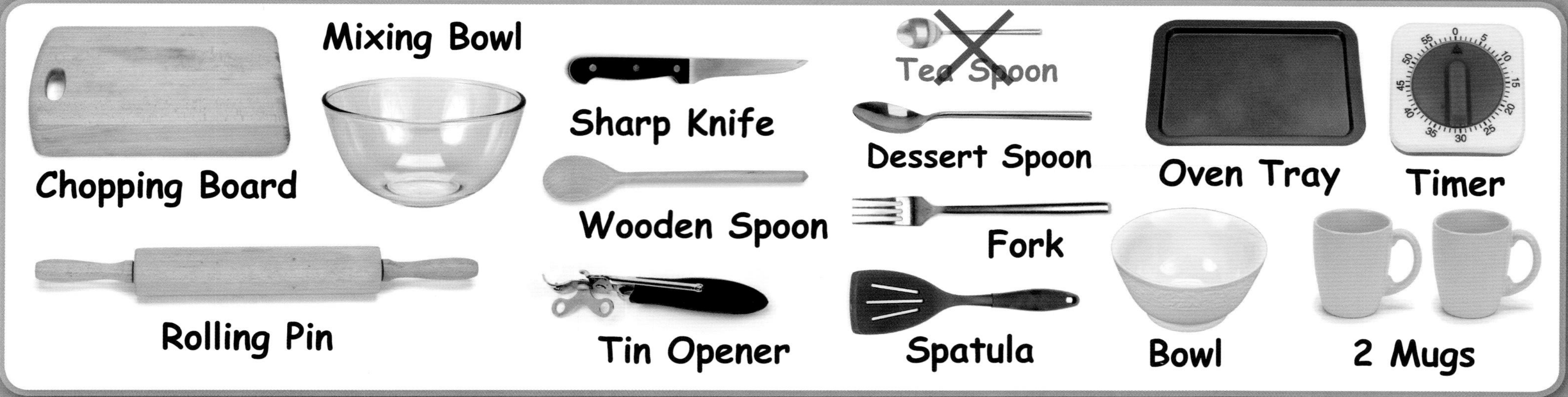
Chopping Board
Rolling Pin
Mixing Bowl
Sharp Knife
Wooden Spoon
Tin Opener
~~Tea Spoon~~
Dessert Spoon
Fork
Spatula
Oven Tray
Bowl
Timer
2 Mugs

Pizza

1
200°C 400°F Gas mark 6

2
Plain Flour
Full Mug

3
Plain Flour
½ Mug

4

5
SALT

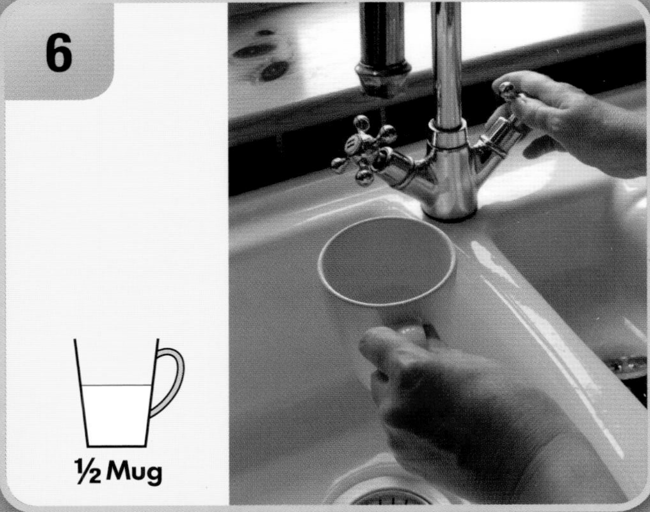
6
½ Mug

Pizza

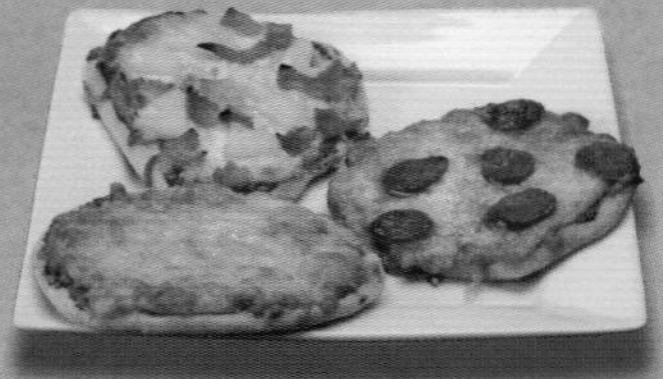

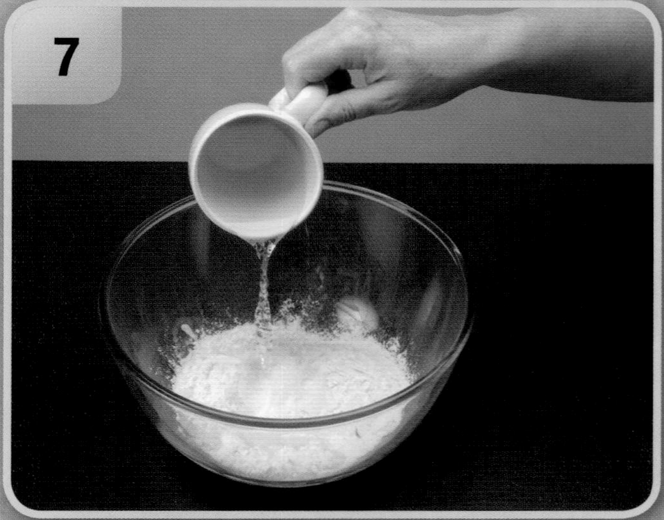
7

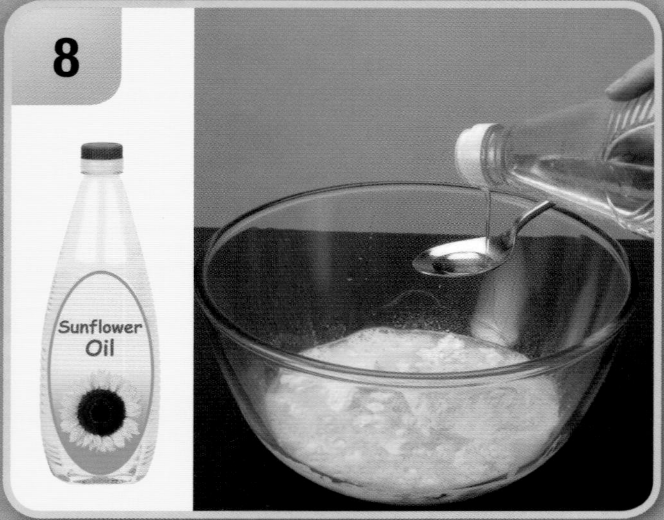
8
Sunflower
Oil

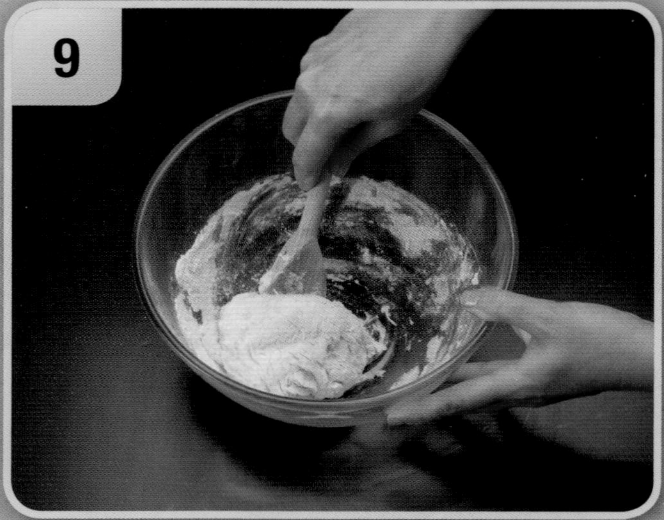
9

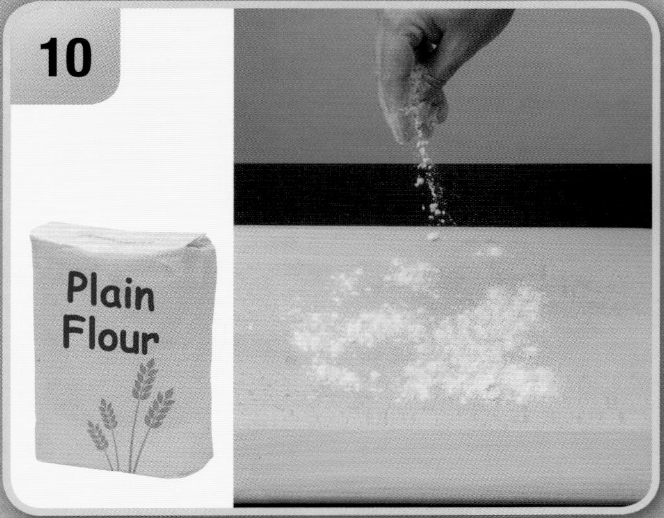
10
Plain
Flour

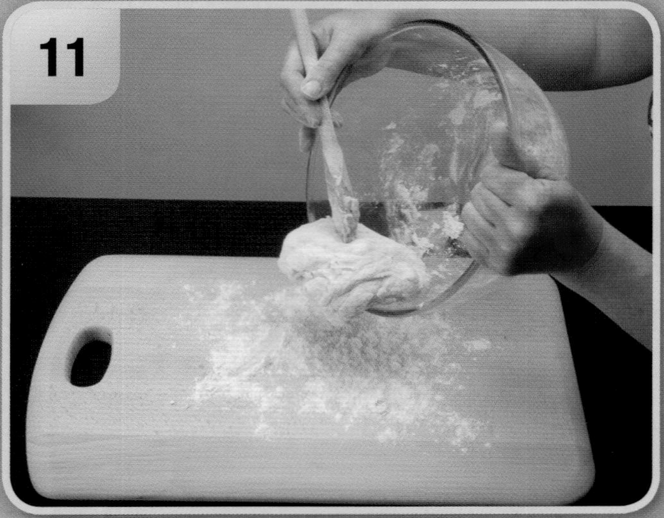
11

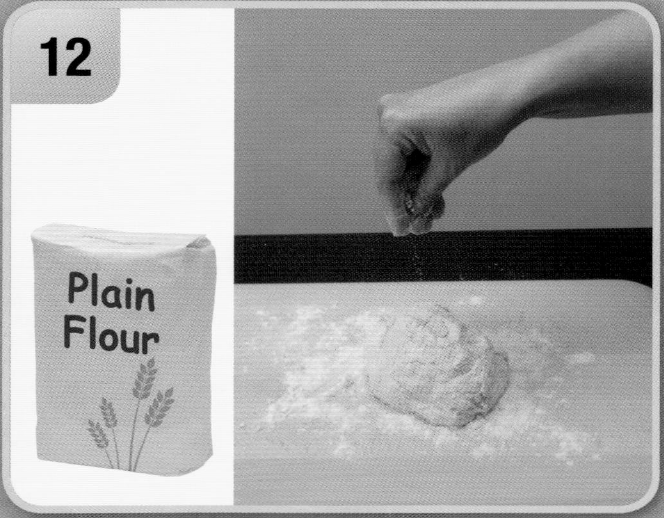
12
Plain
Flour

Pizza

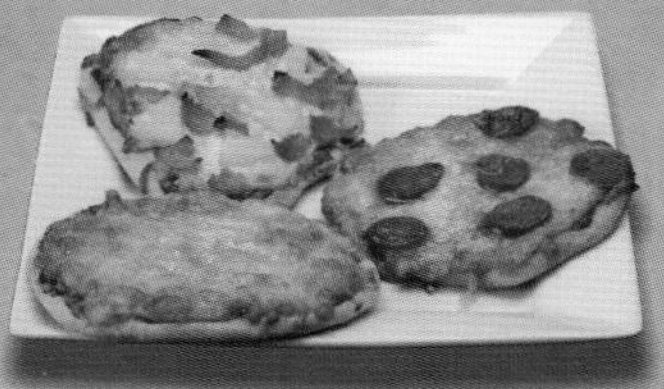

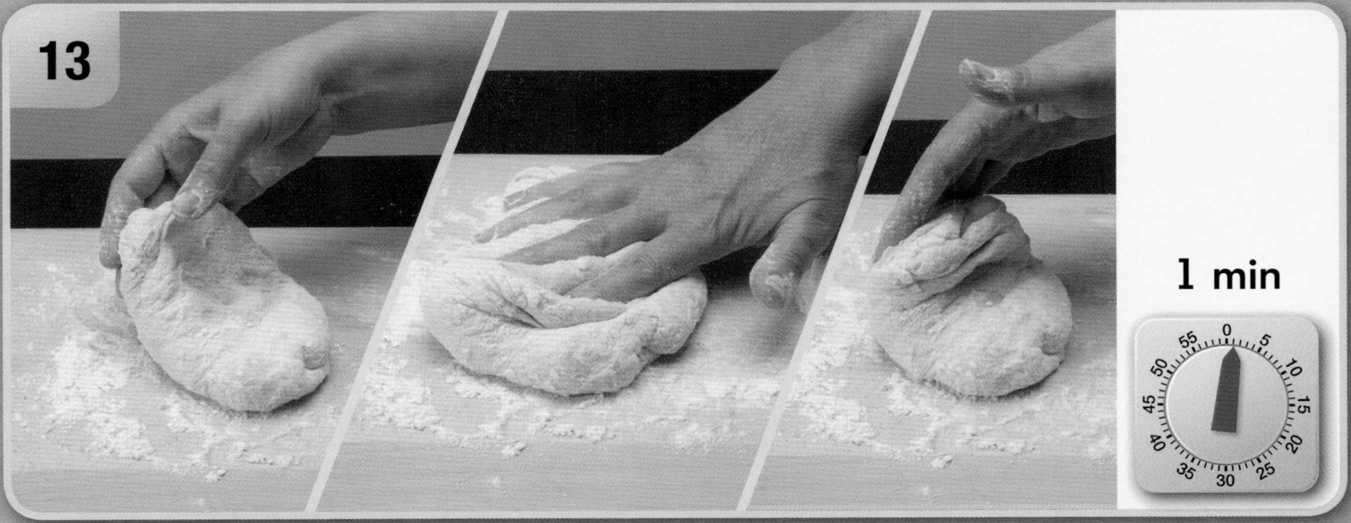
13
1 min

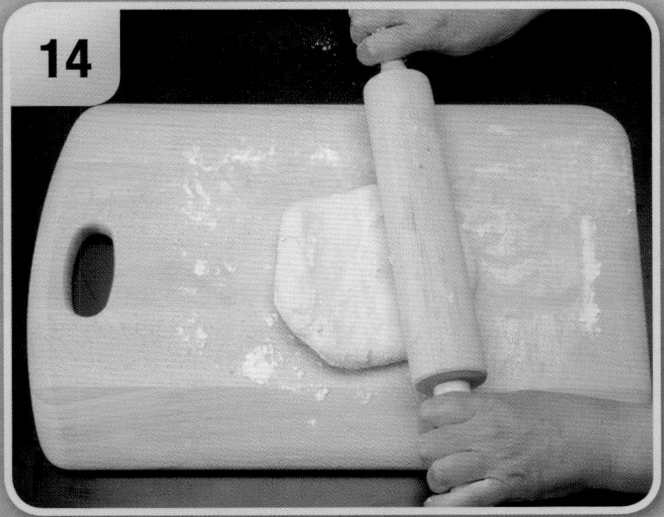
14

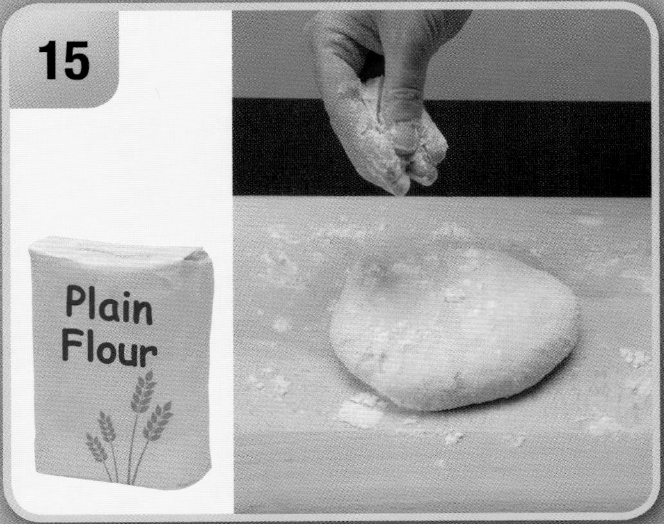
15
Plain Flour

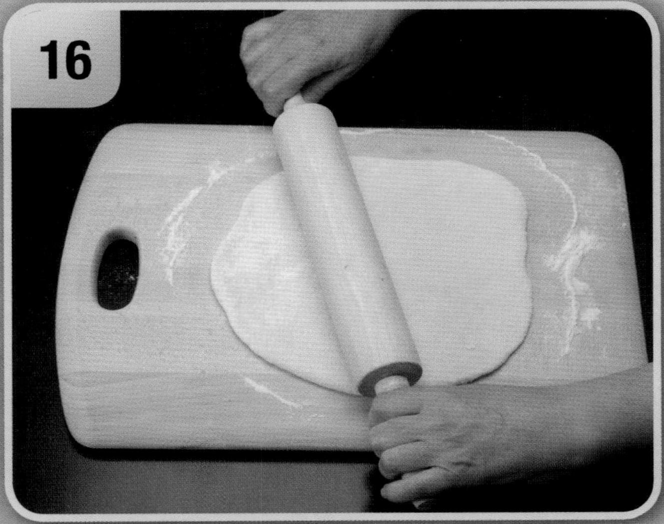
16

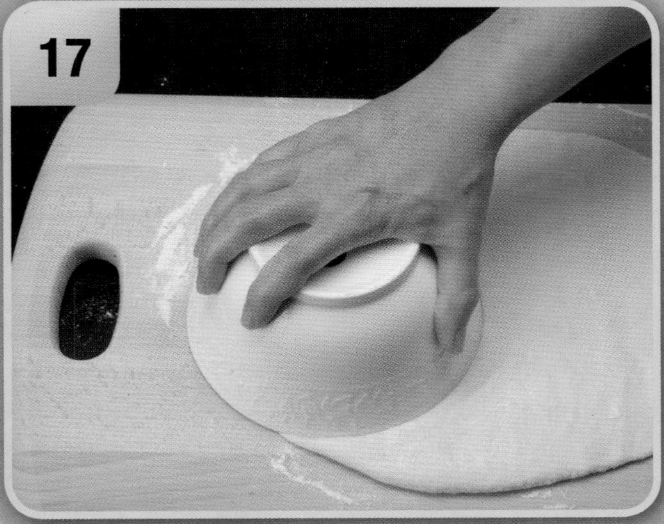
17

Pizza

Pizza

24
Tomato Purée

25

26
Grated Cheese

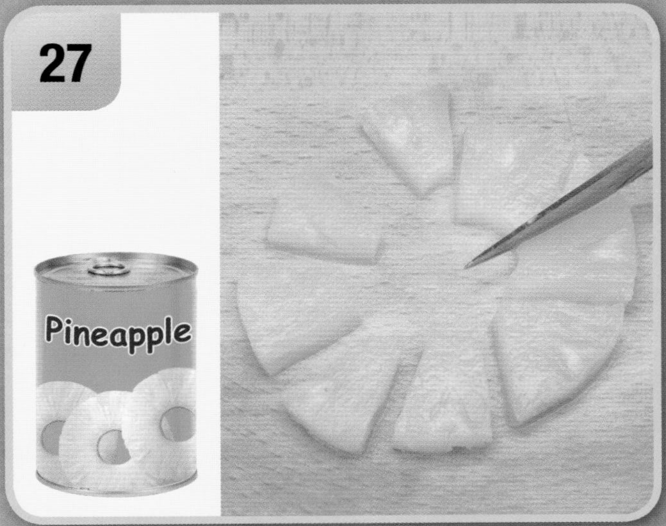
27
Pineapple

28
Chorizo Sausage

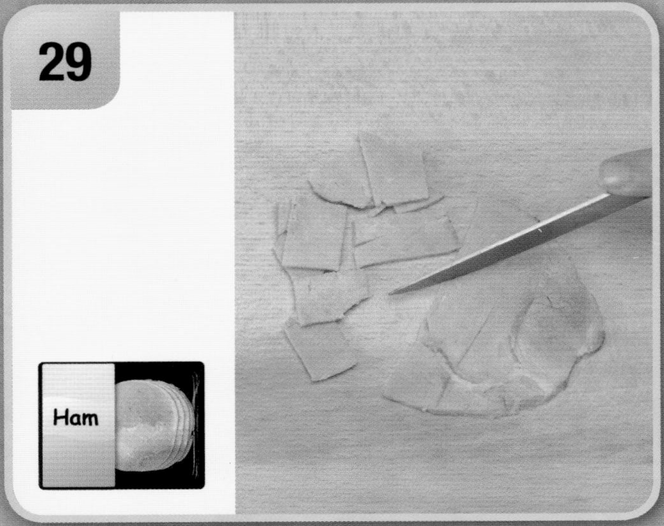
29
Ham

Pizza

30

31

32

Shepherd's Pie

500g Mince

Mushrooms

6 Potatoes

1 Carrot

Butter

1 Red Pepper

1 Onion

Tin of Beans

Salt

Tomato Ketchup

Packet of Shepherd's Pie Mix

Frying Pan

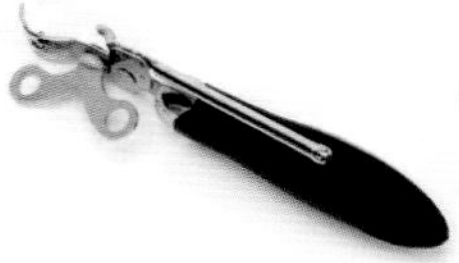

Tea Spoon

Dessert Spoon

Saucepan

Sharp Knife

Potato Masher

Colander

Tin Opener

Chopping Board

Spatula

Oven Dish

Mug

Timer

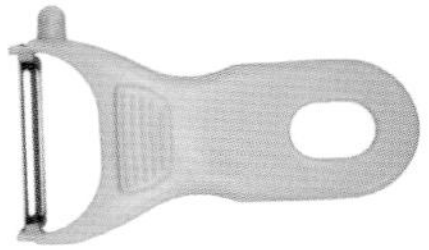

Potato Peeler

Shepherd's Pie

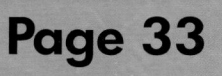

Shepherd's Pie

7

8

9

10

11

12

200°C 400°F Gas mark 6

Shepherd's Pie

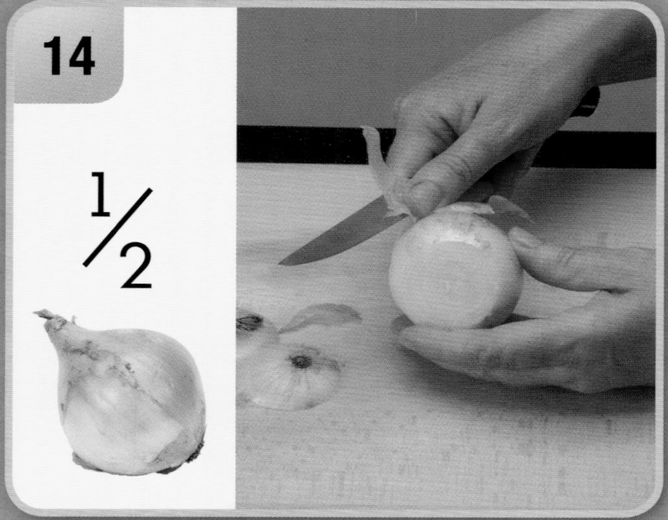

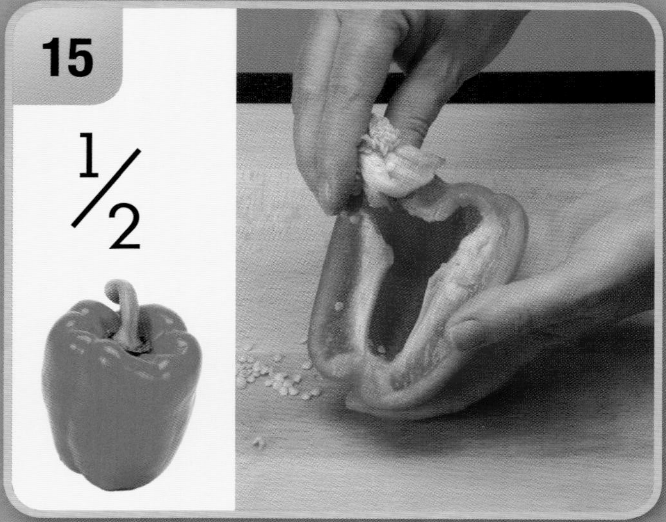

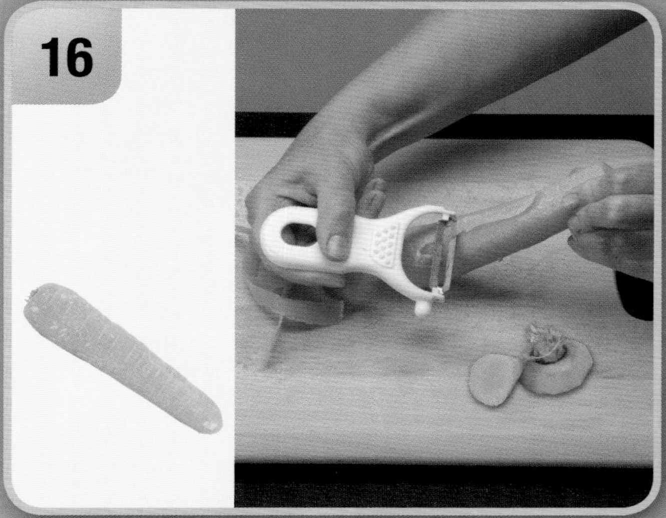

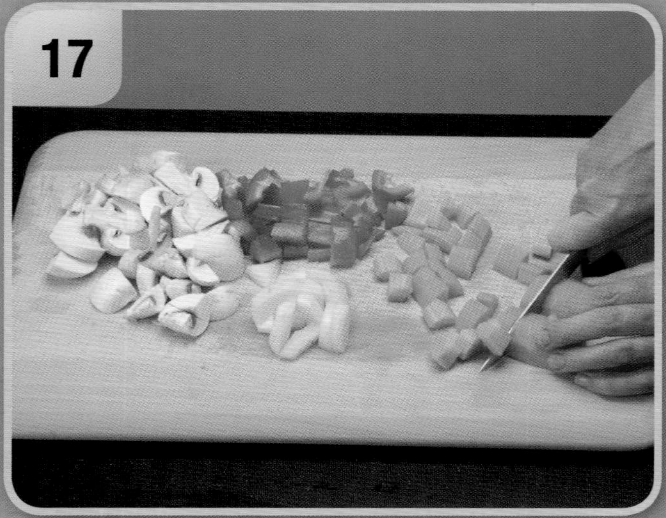

Shepherd's Pie

19

20

21

22

23

24

Shepherd's Pie

25

26

½

5 mins

27

28

29

30 mins

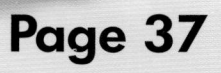

Spaghetti Bolognese

500g Mince

Salt

Tin of Tomatoes

Mushrooms

Tomato Puree

1 Red Pepper

Jar of Bolognese Sauce

1 Onion

Spaghetti

2 Saucepans

Chopping Board

Spatula

Frying Pan

Timer

~~Tea Spoon~~

Wooden Spoon

Dessert Spoon

Sharp Knife

Tin Opener

Colander

Spaghetti Bolognese

Spaghetti Bolognese

Spaghetti Bolognese

13

14

15

16

17

18

Spaghetti Bolognese

Chicken Curry and Rice

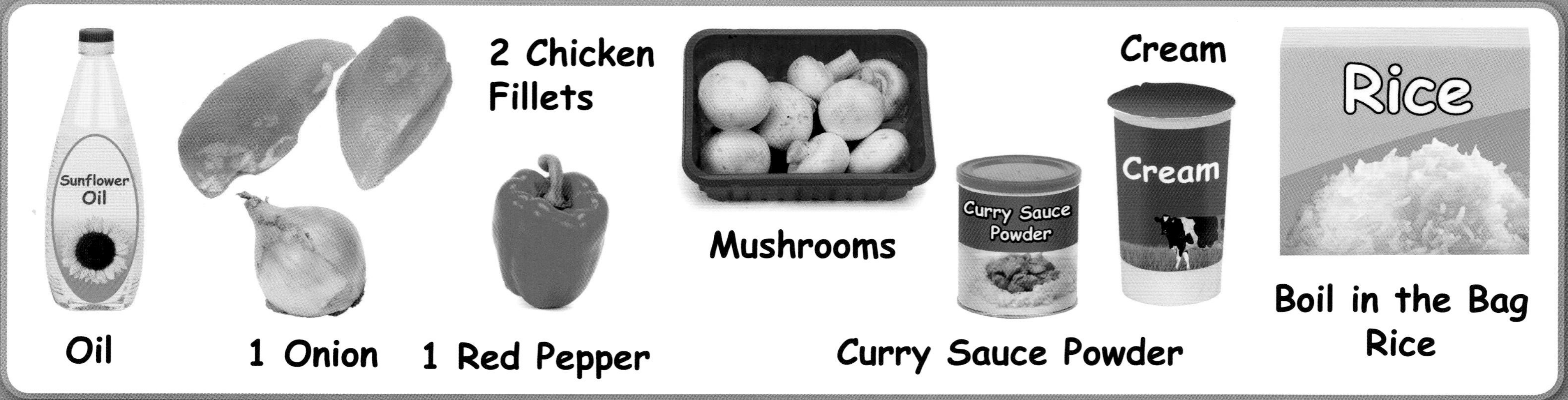
Sunflower Oil
Oil
2 Chicken Fillets
1 Onion
1 Red Pepper
Mushrooms
Curry Sauce Powder
Curry Sauce Powder
Cream
Cream
Rice
Boil in the Bag Rice

2 Saucepans
Frying Pan
Tea Spoon
Whisk
Dessert Spoon
Spatula
Sharp Knife
2 Chopping Boards
Colander
Timer
2 Mugs

Chicken Curry and Rice

1

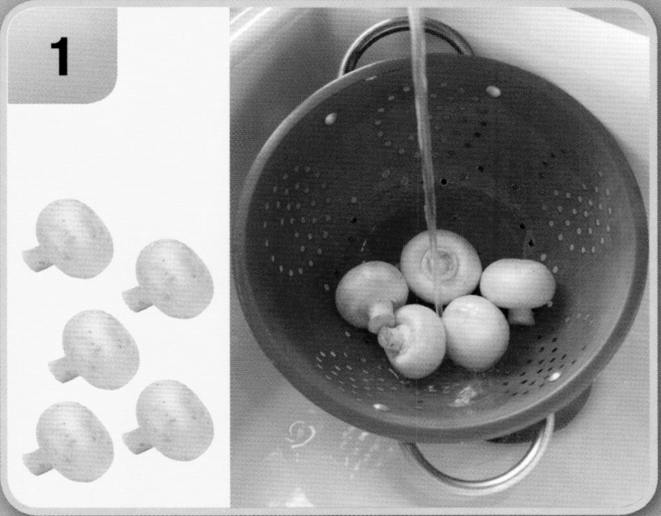

2

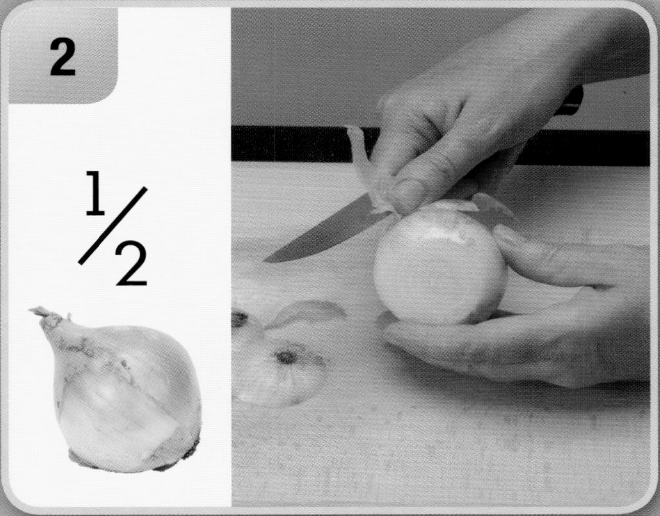

3

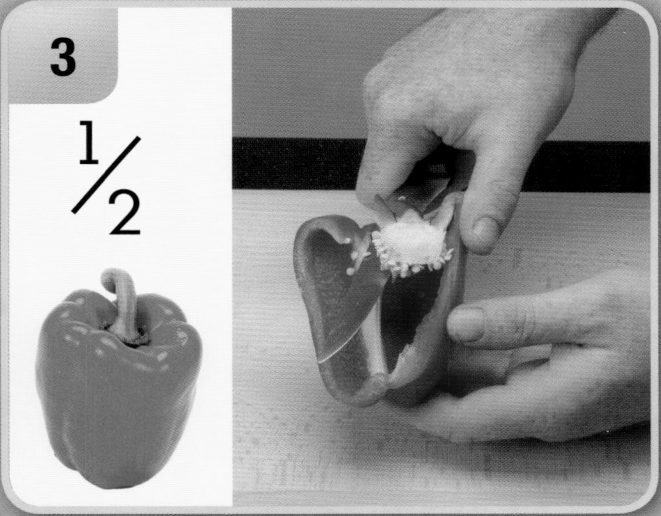

4

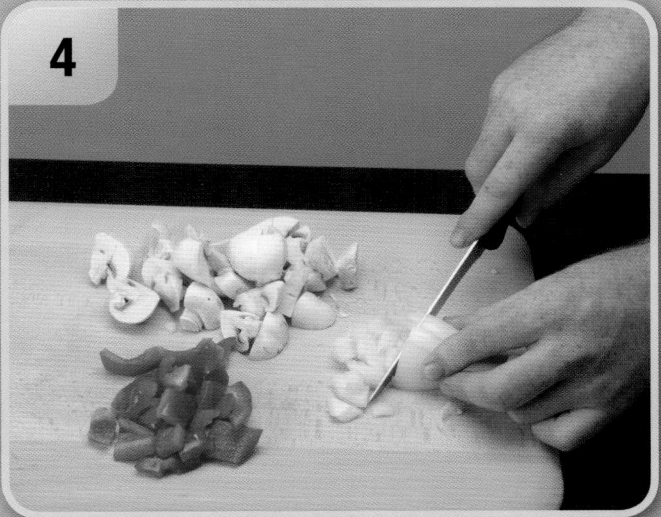

5

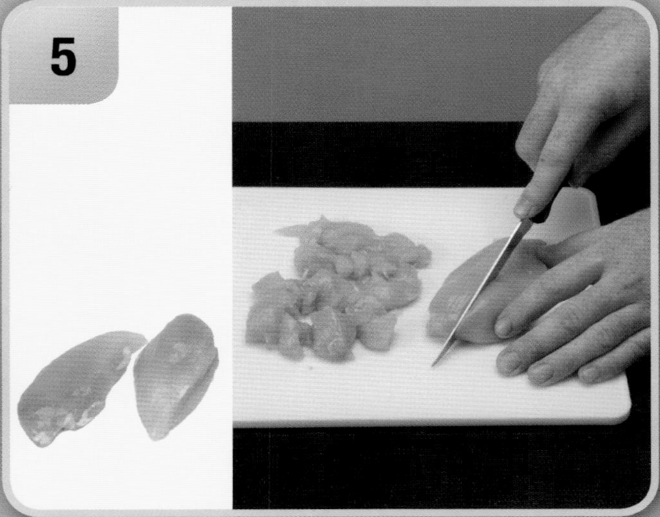

6

Chicken Curry and Rice

Chicken Curry and Rice

Chicken Curry and Rice

Chicken Curry and Rice

Chicken Maryland / Fillet Roll / Fillet Burger

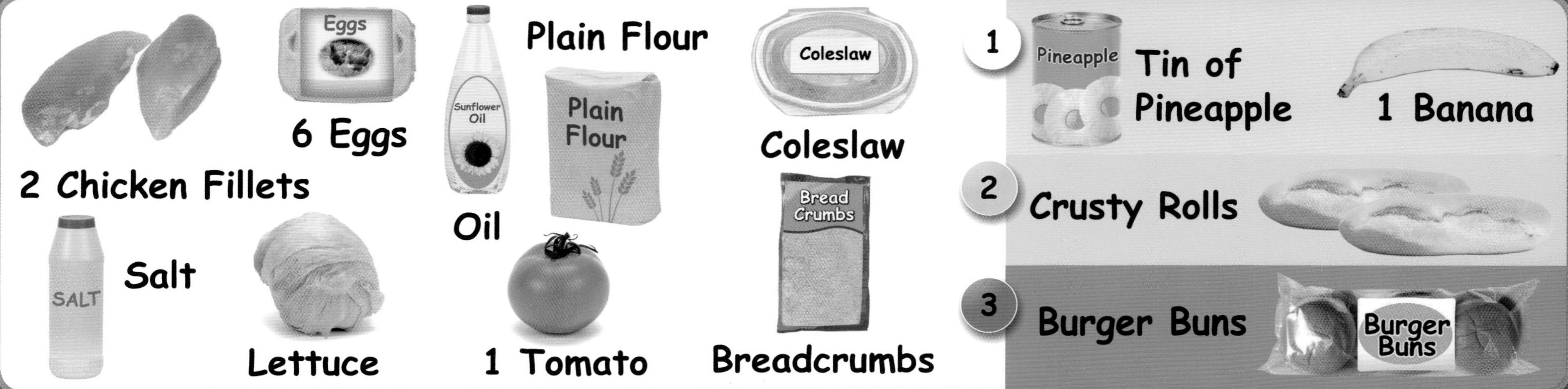

2 Chicken Fillets
6 Eggs
Oil
Plain Flour
Coleslaw
Salt
Lettuce
1 Tomato
Breadcrumbs

1 Tin of Pineapple
1 Banana

2 Crusty Rolls

3 Burger Buns

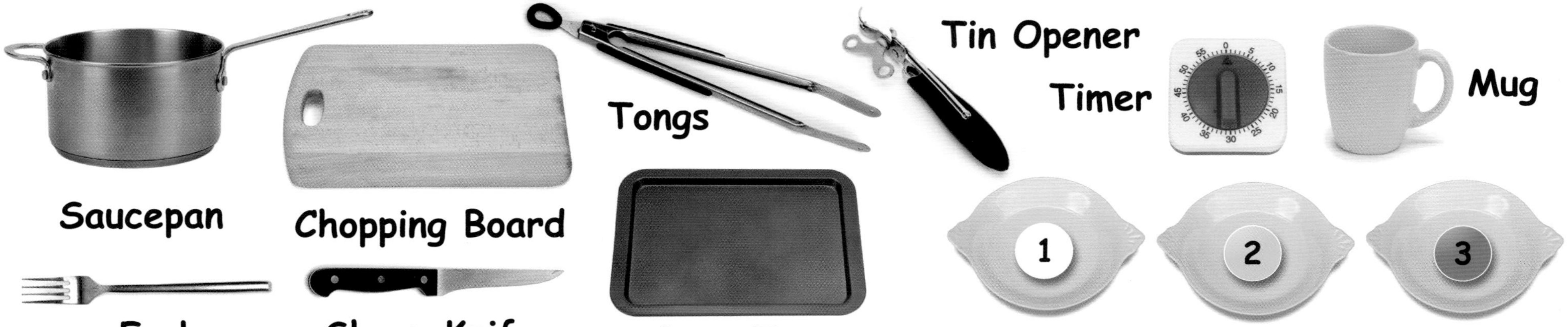

Saucepan
Chopping Board
Tongs
Tin Opener
Timer
Mug
Fork
Sharp Knife
Oven Tray
3 dishes

Chicken Maryland / Fillet Roll / Fillet Burger

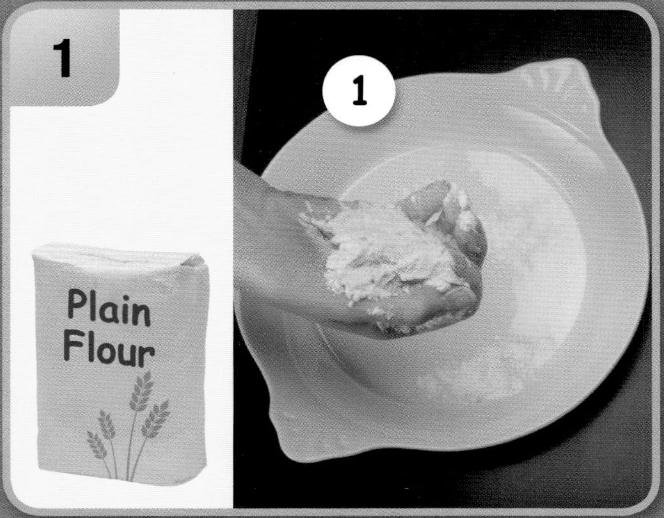

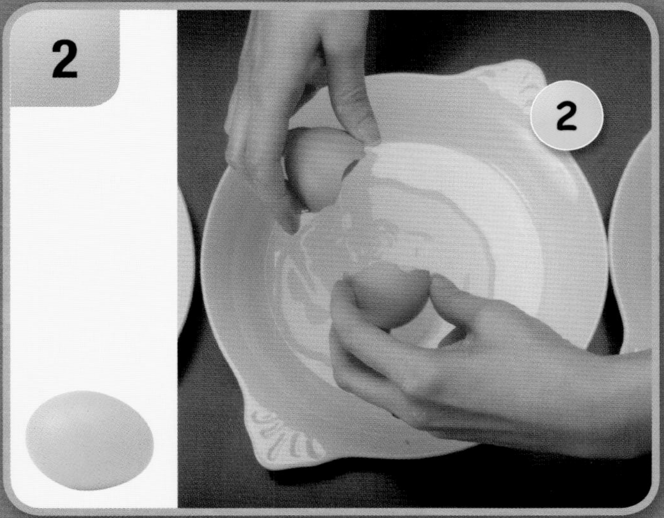

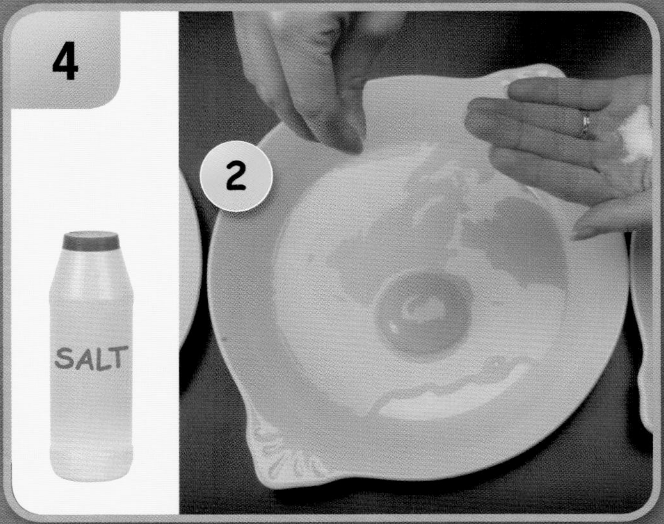

Chicken Maryland / Fillet Roll / Fillet Burger

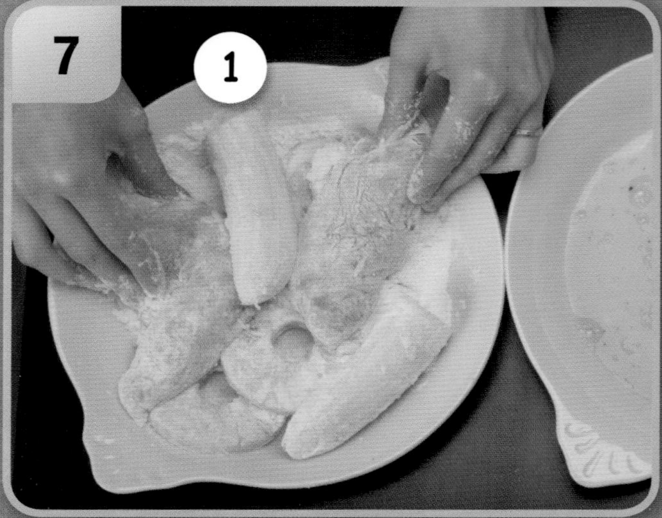

200°C 400°F Gas mark 6

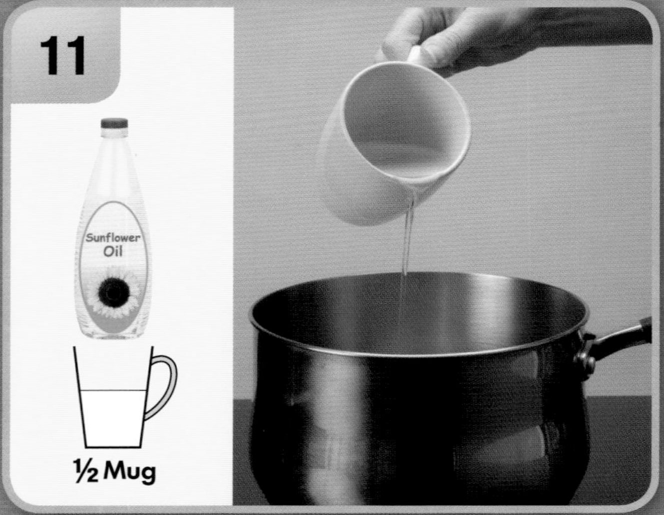

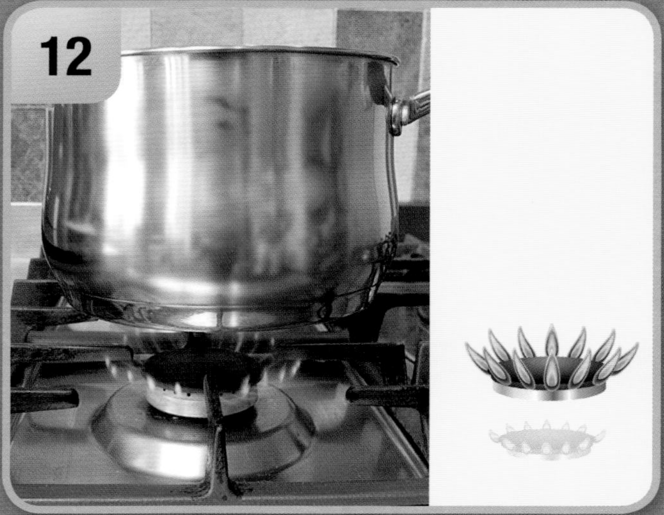

Chicken Maryland / Fillet Roll / Fillet Burger

Chicken Maryland / Fillet Roll / Fillet Burger

Pancakes

Self Raising Flour

6 Eggs

Margarine

Sugar

Milk

~~Tea Spoon~~

Dessert Spoon

Butter Knife

Jug

Frying Pan

Spatula

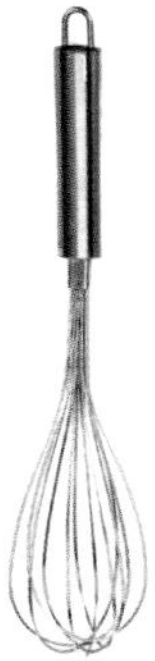

Whisk

Mug

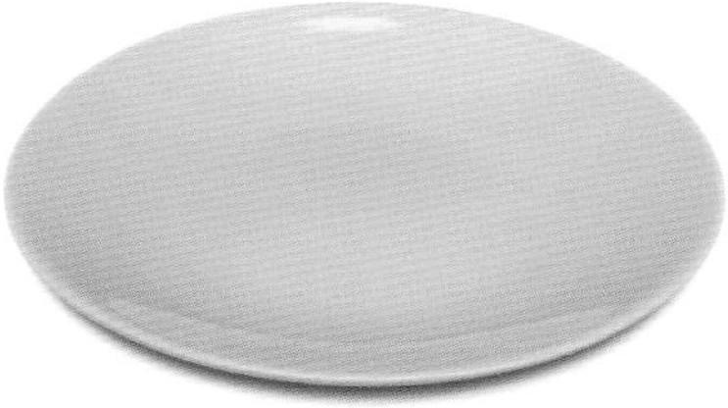

Large Plate

Pancakes

1

2

3

4

5

6

Pancakes

7

8

9

10

11

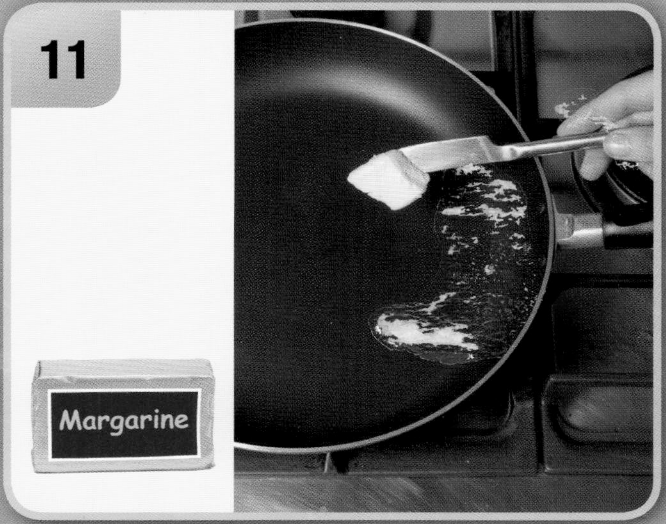

12

Pancakes

13

14

15

16

11 > 16

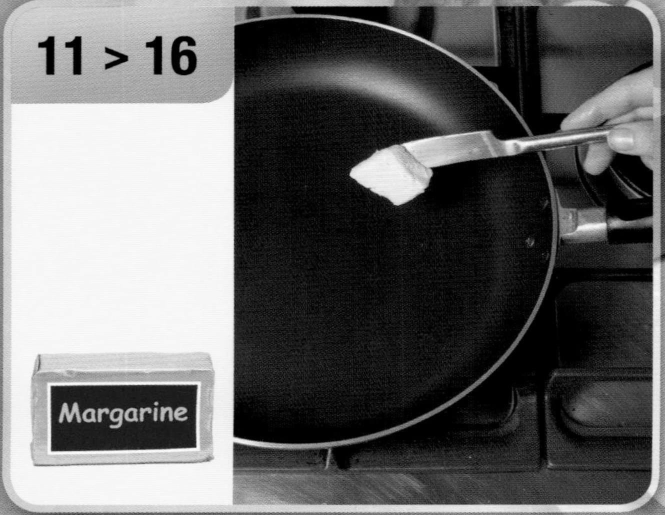

Scrambled Egg and Toast

6 Eggs

Salt

Black Pepper

Milk

Block of Cheese

Butter

Bread

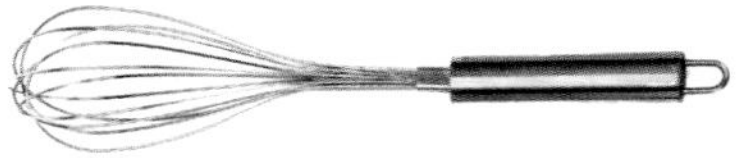
Whisk

Butter Knife

Bowl

Plate

Egg Cup

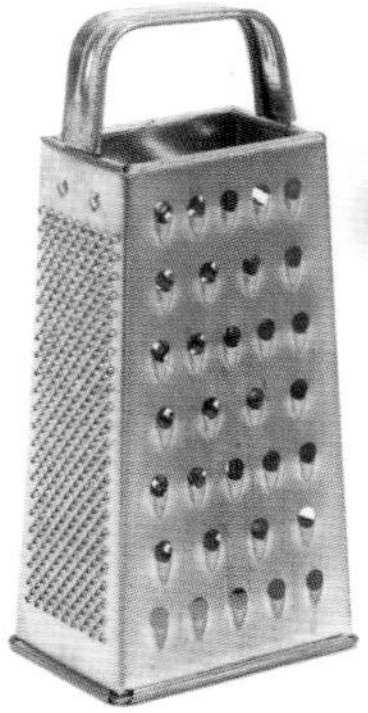
Grater

Frying Pan

Spatula

Scrambled Egg and Toast

1

2

3

4

5

6

Scrambled Egg and Toast

7

8

9

10

11

12

Scrambled Egg and Toast

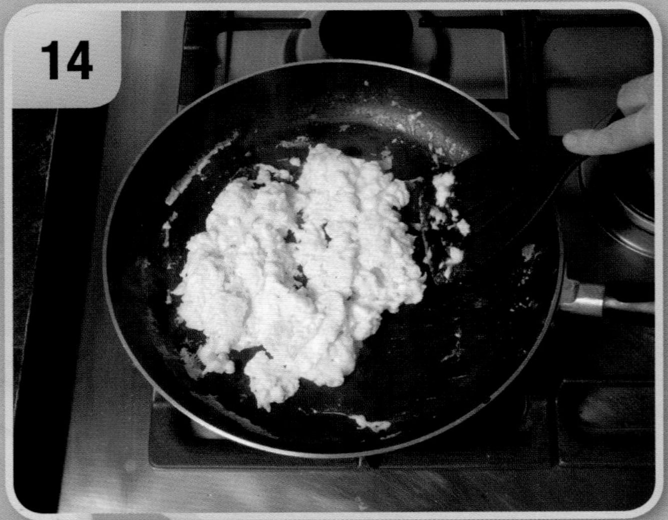

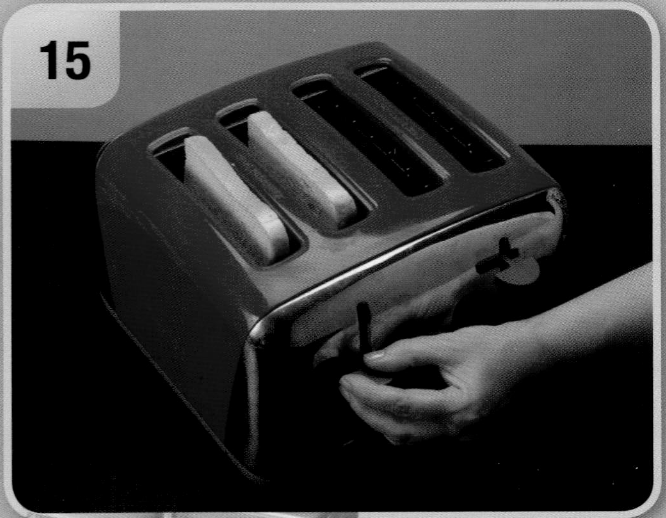

French Toast

6 Eggs

Salt

Milk

Butter

Bread

Black Pepper

Dish

Whisk

Butter Knife

Egg Cup

Frying Pan

Spatula

Plate

French Toast

French Toast

French Toast

13

14

Apple Crumble and Custard

3 Cooking Apples

Margarine

Ready to Pour Custard

Self Raising Flour

Sugar

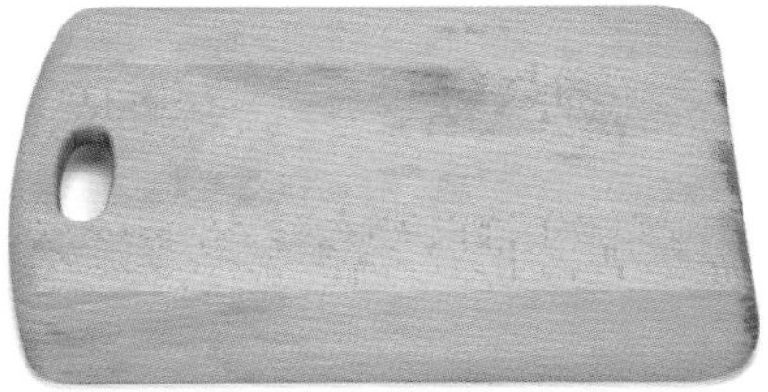

Chopping Board

Sharp Knife

2 Mugs

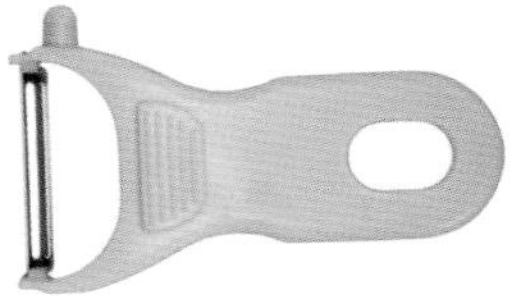

Potato Peeler

Timer

Mixing Bowl

Oven Dish

Tea Spoon

Dessert Spoon

Apple Crumble and Custard

1

200°C 400°F Gas mark 6

2

3

4

5

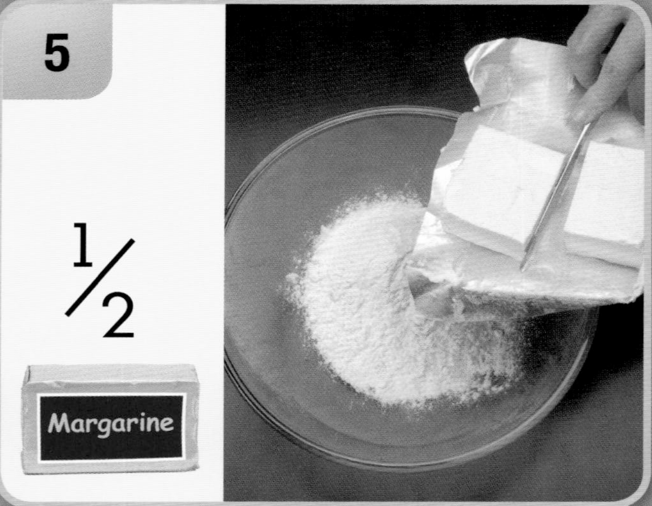

6

Apple Crumble and Custard

7

8

9

10

11

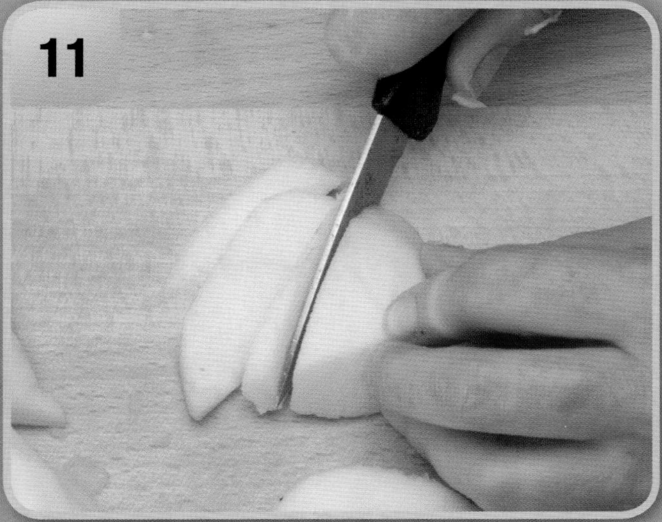

12

Apple Crumble and Custard

13

14

15

16

17

Strawberry Cheesecake

Digestive Biscuits

2 Plastic Bags

Tin of Strawberries

227g Butter

Packet Strawberry Jelly

200g Soft Cheese

284ml Cream

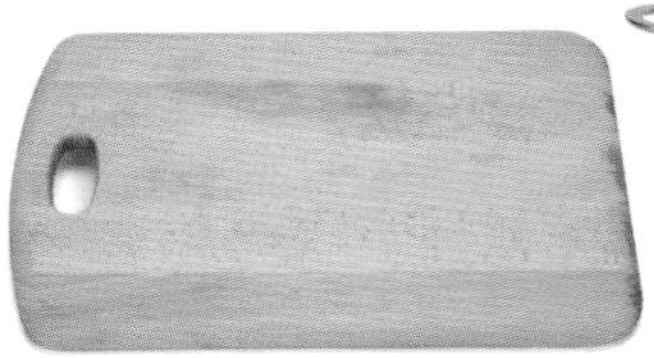

Chopping Board

2 Saucepans

Sharp Knife

Mixing Bowl

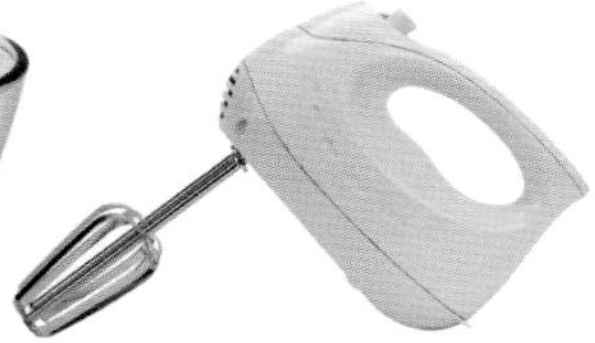

Food Mixer

Colander

Timer

~~Tea Spoon~~

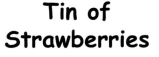

Rolling Pin

Flan Dish

Spatula

Tin Opener

Wooden Spoon

Dessert Spoon

Strawberry Cheesecake

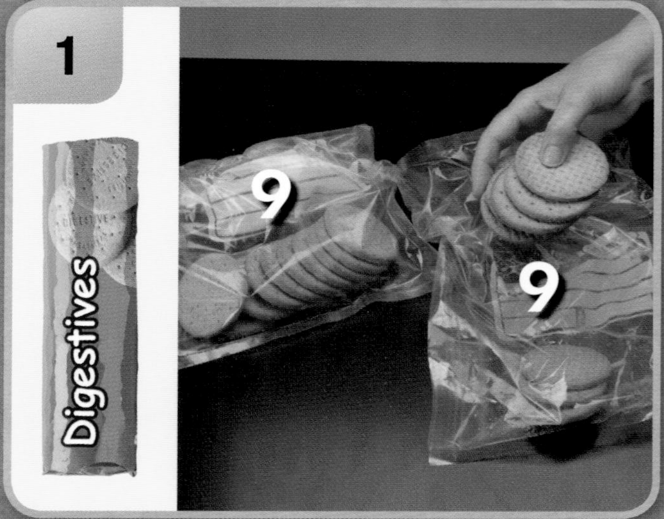

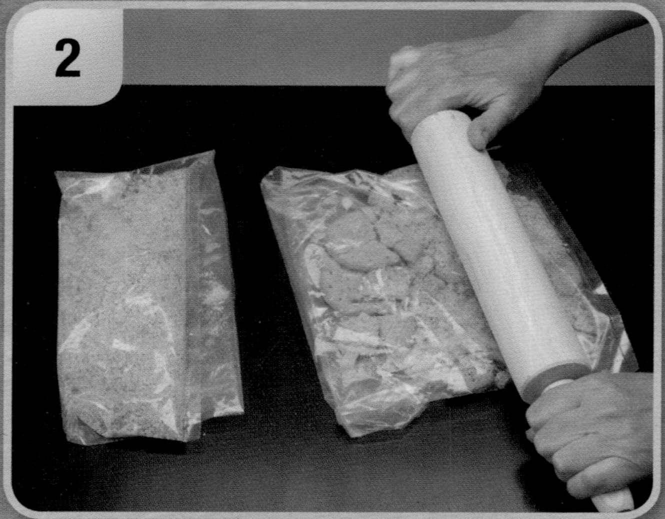

Strawberry Cheesecake

Strawberry Cheesecake

13

14

15

16

17

18

Strawberry Cheesecake

Buns

2 Mugs

Mixer

Sieve

Butter Knife

Spatula

Dessert Spoon

Tea Spoon

Timer

Mixing Bowl

Wire Tray

Egg Cup

Small Bowl

2 Bun Tins

Saucepan

Cream

Icing Sugar

Sugar Strands

Cooking Chocolate

Milk

Cornflour

Caster Sugar

Margarine

To Decorate:

Bun Cases

6 Eggs

Baking Powder

Self Raising Flour

Buns

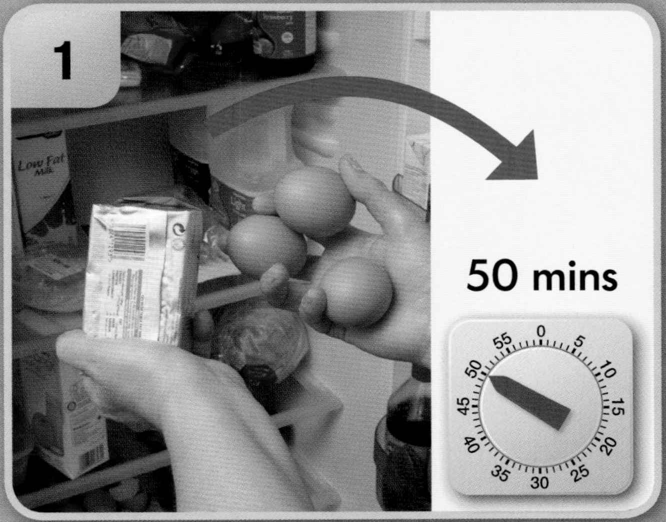
1
50 mins

2
200°C 400°F Gas mark 6

3
Self Raising Flour
Full Mug

4
Self Raising Flour
½ Mug

5

6
Caster Sugar
½ Mug

Buns

7

8
Tea Spoon
Cornflour

9
Tea Spoon
Baking Powder

10

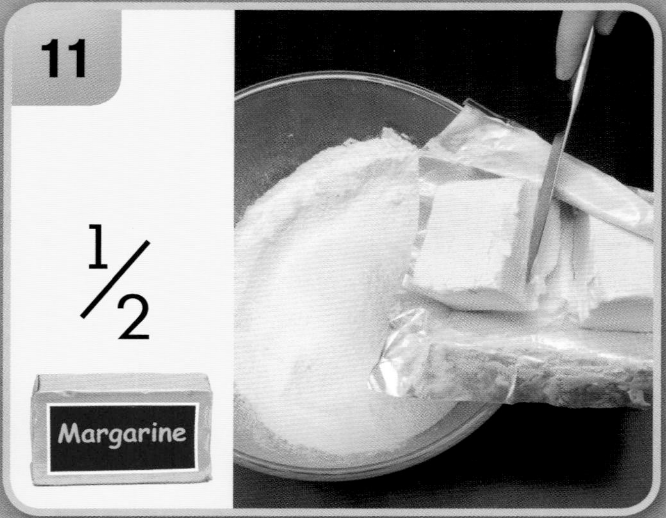
11
1/2
Margarine

12

Buns

13

14

15

16

17

18

Buns

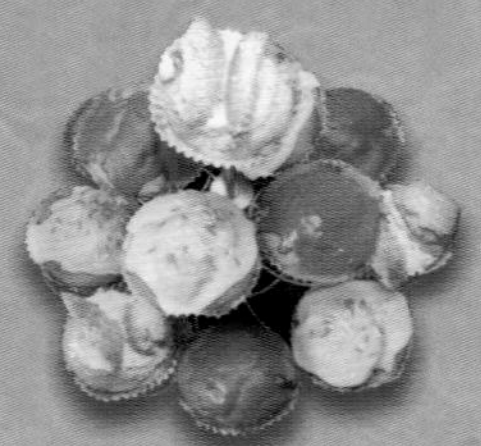

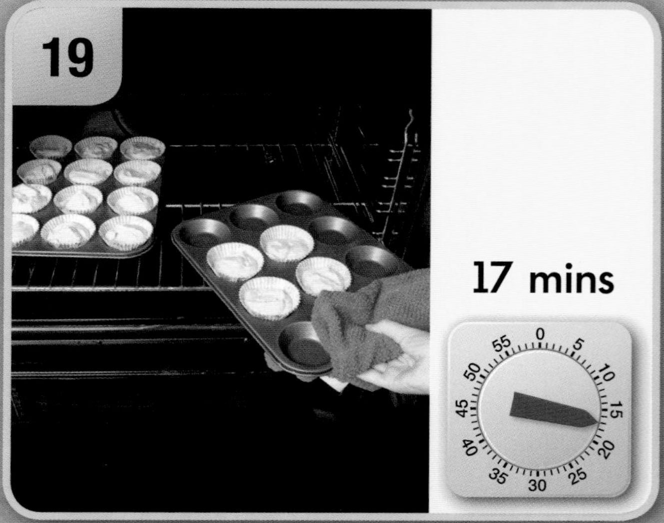
19
17 mins

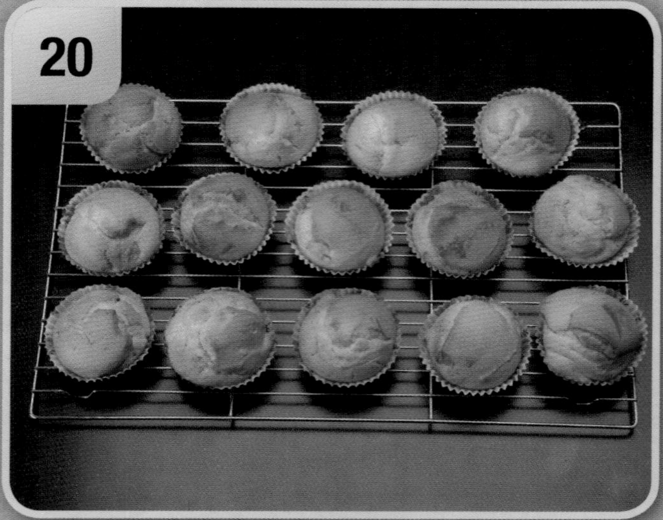
20

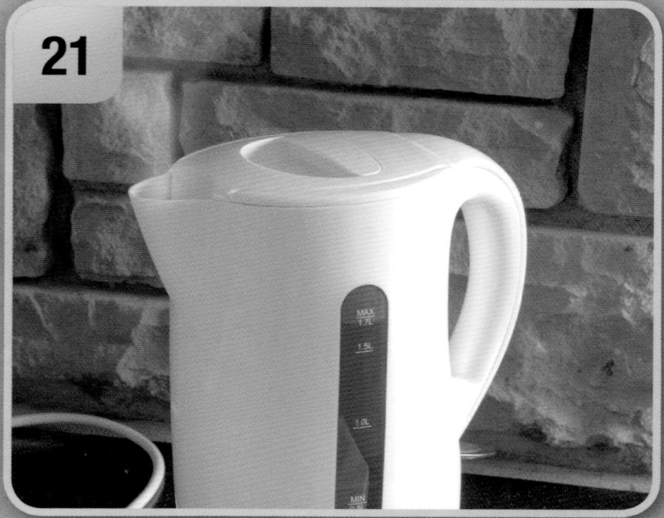
21

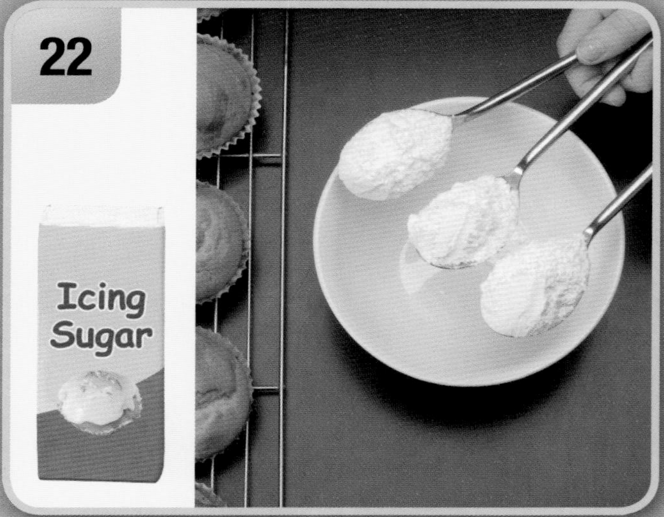
22
Icing
Sugar

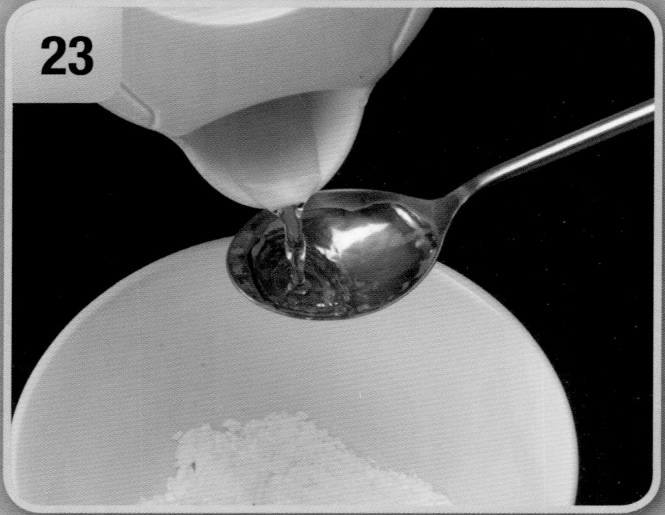
23

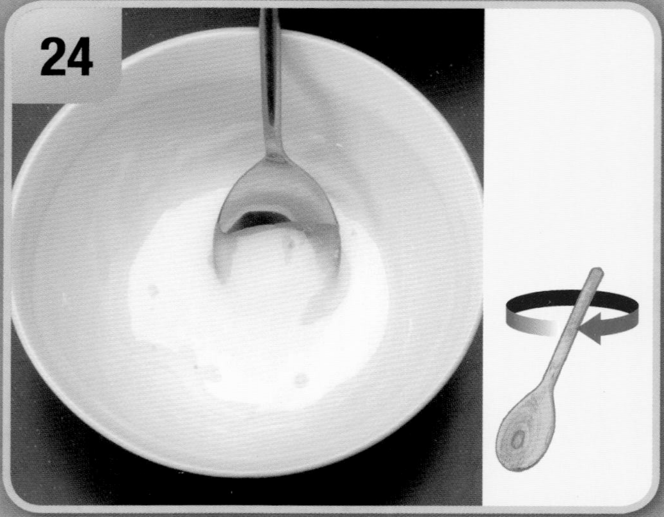
24

Buns

25

26

27

28

29

30

Buns

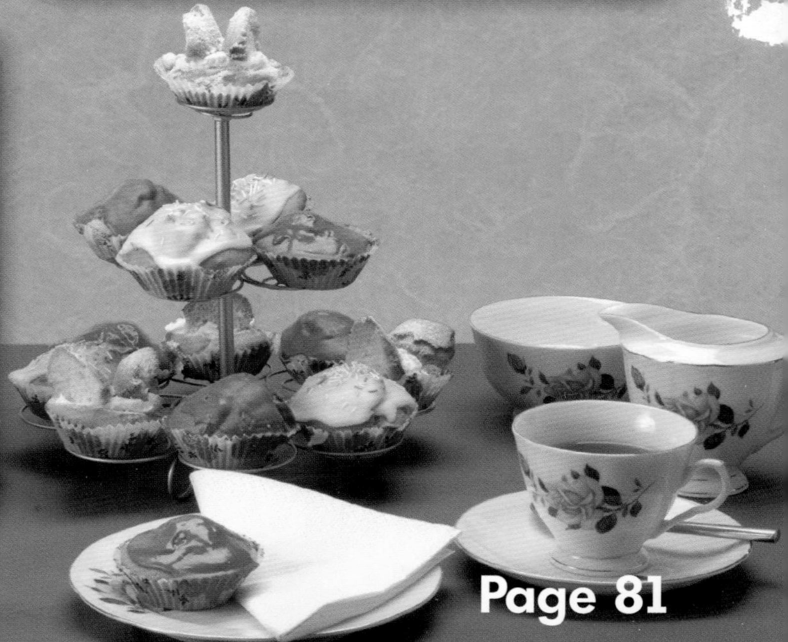

I would love to hear how you are getting on using this book.

Have you got a nice story to share?

Have you any particular favourite recipes that you like to cook?

Have you any dish that you would like to see included in the next book?

Go on leave a comment on
www.justlookandcook.ie

or Join me on Facebook at **Just Look and Cook**

A day in the life of a cookery book photo shoot...